Firm Foundations

'An experienced preacher allows us into his study, even his thoughts, as he prepares his sermons. By his own admission he is 'a linear progressive thinker and preacher'. This is particularly useful since in the outlines that form the major part of this book we benefit from his clear and systematic structures which highlight issues that may be addressed even if the outline itself is not followed. The introduction of recommended books is also very helpful. This is not a volume of instant sermon solutions! Preaching is work. *Firm Foundations* is another valuable tool for the workshop.'
Bev Savage, General Secretary of the Fellowship of Independent Evangelical Churches

'At the turn of the last century Sangster, the renowned Methodist preacher in London declared, "preaching is in the shadows, the world does not believe in it." A century later the situation is graver still. Large segments of the church apparently do not believe that expository preaching is crucial to the health of God's people.

Peter Grainger's *Firm Foundations* sounds a loud and clear note for lively, imaginative, Bible-based, Christ-centered preaching. These principles and patterns will prove as helpful to the seasoned expositor as they will to the fledgling pastor. I commend it enthusiastically.'
Alistair Begg, Pastor, Parkside Church, Ohio

'Both aspiring and established preachers are intrigued to know how other preachers go about their task. Besides the excellent and practical introduction on preparing to preach, this book provides invaluable insight, through its numerous outline sermons, into the importance of structure and variety. While each individual must develop an entirely personal style and approach, none can fail to be stimulated in the right direction by what this book provides. It fills a definite gap in contemporary books on preaching.'
Derek Prime
Retired Minister of Charlotte Baptist Chapel

'Reading *Firm Foundations* is a little like reading Donald Grey *Barnhouse's Let Me Illustrate*. The value is not that you or I would ever preach these sermons— any more than we would repeat Barnhouse's illustrations. Grainger's approach to preaching and sermons are both distinctively his. Rather the value is in getting a glimpse into the mind and heart of someone who expounds Scripture well in his setting. Like a good sermon illustration, the specificity of this book, with its many introductions and outlines, helps us who preach imagine how we could craft our sermons and sermon series that are equally faithful to Scripture.'
Greg R. Scharf, Associate Professor and Chair of Practical Theology
Trinity Evangelical Divinity School, Deerfield, Illinois, USA

Firm Foundations

150 examples of how to structure a sermon

Peter Grainger

Christian Focus

Christian Focus Publications
publishes books for all ages

Our mission statement –

STAYING FAITHFUL

In dependence upon God we seek to help make His infallible word, the Bible, relevant. Our aim is to ensure that the Lord Jesus Christ is presented as the only hope to obtain forgiveness of sin, live a useful life and look forward to heaven with Him.

REACHING OUT

Christ's last command requires us to reach out to our world with His gospel. We seek to help fulfill that by publishing books that point people towards Jesus and help them to develop a Christ-like maturity. We aim to equip all levels of readers for life, work, ministry and mission.

Books in our adult range are published in three imprints.

Christian Focus contains popular works including biographies, commentaries, basic doctrine, and Christian living. Our children's books are also published in this imprint.

Mentor focuses on books written at a level suitable for Bible College and seminary students, pastors, and other serious readers. The imprint includes commentaries, doctrinal studies, examination of current issues, and church history.

Christian Heritage contains classic writings from the past.

ISBN 1–85792–678–1

© Copyright Peter Grainger 2003

Published in 2003
by
Christian Focus Publications, Ltd.
Geanies House, Fearn, Tain,
Ross–shire, IV20 1TW, Great Britain.

www.christianfocus.com

Cover Design by Alister MacInnes

Printed and bound by
Mackays of Chatham

Contents

Foreword

The church which is now known as Charlotte Chapel was founded in another part of Edinburgh in 1808. A few years earlier, a young Edinburgh businessman had heard and responded to a call to join William Carey, the 'first modern missionary', in Serampore in India. As he neared the completion of his preparations to sail for India, it was decided, and he very reluctantly accepted, that his health would not stand a tropical climate. Christopher Anderson returned to his native city and began evangelistic outreach in one of the un–churched suburbs. Eighteen months later, those who had come to faith in Christ through his ministry invited him to constitute them as a church and to be their pastor.

At this time, the City of Edinburgh was expanding rapidly into the area we know as the 'New Town'. The Scottish Episcopalians secured a site for a church, 'next to South Charlotte Street, to be called Charlotte Chapel', both named after the Queen of the day. Through preaching by illustrious visitors and the steady work of the minister, Bishop Sandford, the congregation grew until by 1814 the 700 seats in the one–storey building were no longer sufficient. They moved across Princes Street to St John's, the magnificent edifice which still graces the west end of Princes Street.

Christopher Anderson seized the opportunity of purchasing their building in the heart of the New Town. He kept the name Charlotte Chapel but since 'Chapels' in Scotland are generally places of worship for Roman Catholics – the English pairing of 'church and chapel' has no parallel here – members tended to call it 'Charlotte Baptist Chapel'. Christopher Anderson's preaching attracted 'all denominations in the evenings, people of the best rank in society' – not many other churches had a Sunday evening service in those days. The building was regularly filled to overflowing and one visiting clergyman left a card in his seat, 'Rev. F– B–, Rector of F–, has listened with delight to the very faithful preaching of the Gospel this evening.'

Christopher Anderson was the first of many 'expository preachers' in Charlotte Chapel.

He first laid open the whole passage in its connection to full view, in few words, and then at greater length drew out the spirit of the writer, or rather 'the mind of the Spirit,' from the various clauses, applying the whole to the circumstances of the believer at the present time. We might instance some of his lectures on our Lord's parables, and on the epistles to the seven churches in Asia, which were listened to with interest and delight. His preference for exposition, and the textual mode of preaching in general, arose naturally out of his love for the letter of the Bible, from which he drew the spirit.

He was the sole pastor until 1851. There followed a succession of fairly short pastorates and at the end of the nineteenth century there was serious talk of closing the doors for good. However, the new pastor, Rev. Joseph Kemp, called the small congregation to fervent and continuous prayer, devoted the morning service to expository preaching and the evening service to evangelism. Crowds queued for a seat and soon the building was inadequate for the numbers who wanted to attend. The old building was demolished and the present one erected on the same site in 1912. The members wholeheartedly supported and supplemented the evangelistic pulpit ministry – an Edinburgh clergyman, not a Baptist, told a story against himself after he visited one of these Sunday evening services. Between the benediction and his reaching the door, no less than five separate members of the Chapel asked him if he was 'saved', so he commented wryly that he must have appeared to be in great need of salvation.

Rapid expansion throughout Joseph Kemp's years presented the Chapel with a challenge, which was to build up its members in their new-found faith. For this, a ministry of systematic teaching was needed and was met by the 17 year pastorate of Rev. W. Graham Scroggie, starting in May 1916. Already well-known as a Keswick expositor, he emphasised the importance of inter-action between pulpit and pew in preaching. When he arrived in Edinburgh he said, 'You are looking to me for spiritual instruction. I am looking to you for spiritual inspiration. We are a body and the health and usefulness of the whole depends on every separate part fulfilling its function.' From the pulpit he presented the doctrines of the Christian faith so clearly that the Church Secretary commented, six months later, that his ministry was 'a splendid illustration of the value and fascination of systematic Bible study'. 'The Bible is like a new book', another member commented, 'and we are learning the mind of God from the Word of God and are discovering that this Book is the best thing in the world'.

In 1933 Graham Scroggie resigned from the pastorate of the Chapel, to exercise a ministry to the wider Church in this and other lands. He had stood unreservedly for belief in the whole Bible as the authoritative Word of God, as an organic unity and a Divine Revelation. The same approach to expounding the Scriptures by means of preaching was maintained during Rev. J. Sidlow Baxter's eighteen year pastorate in the Chapel from 1935 to 1953. 'We approach the Bible', said Mr. Baxter, 'as being in its totality the Word of God in our studying of it. Therefore we are seeking to learn under the illumination of the Holy Spirit, the mind and the truth and the will of God'. 'Like his predecessor', commented one hearer, 'Mr. Baxter worked on a broad canvas and his exuberance of thought and spontaneity of expression added joy to our listening'.

The Chapel, which seats 1000, was soon crowded at both services on Sundays. When all the pews were filled, the young people were asked to give up their seats and to perch on the pulpit steps or even in the pulpit itself. Many men, now long past retiring age, still speak fondly of those days when they sat literally at the preacher's feet. Sidlow Baxter's Bible teaching, fresh, penetrating and richly illustrative, was deeply appreciated. He used to say, 'In our study of the Bible, we need ever to guard against becoming so engrossed in the fascination of the subject that we lose sight of the object. Our Lord Jesus Christ Himself has taught us that He is the focal theme of all the Scriptures and everywhere, therefore, we want to see beyond the written Word to Him, who is the Living Word'.

This expository method of preaching, including its practical application to everyday living, was followed by Rev. Gerald B. Griffiths (1954–1961), although from a different theological standpoint. (Graham Scroggie and Sidlow Baxter interpreted Scripture by what is known as 'Dispensationalism', but the popularity of their Bible expositions, both spoken and written, proved that many who did not accept dispensational teaching still derived much benefit from their ministry.) His deep interest in Reformed Theology, and more especially the theology of the Puritans, gave his teaching an emphasis to which Scottish hearers readily responded. His acquaintance with the broad structure of systematic theology, as distinct from Biblical theology, gave to his preaching a balance and proportion that maintained the true reformed emphasis.

Application of spiritual truth to personal experience and conduct was a particularly welcome feature of Gerald Griffith's ministry of the Word. The writer recollects to this day his preaching through the Letter to the Hebrews in 1958, interleaving exposition, explanation and application with memorable phrases like 'the privilege and discipline of bringing up children'.

His successor, Rev. Alan Redpath (1962–1966), was steeped in the Keswick devotional and evangelistic tradition, always seeking a response, always evoking questions in the minds of the congregation. The sermon which the writer best remembers was his exposition of the passage in Matthew 8, where a centurion asked the Saviour to heal his paralysed servant. Demurring when Jesus said that he would visit the patient, and suggesting that the healing could be carried out from where they were, the centurion explained that 'I am a man under authority, with soldiers under me. I tell this one, 'Go' and he goes ...' Alan Redpath drew out the lesson that because the centurion acknowledged a Master (Caesar), he had influence over others, and so we will have spiritual influence and authority in measure as we submit our lives to our Master.

Rev. Derek J. Prime (1969–1987), having learned in his earlier years as a schoolmaster the skill of communication, expounded Book after Book in clear and challenging sermons. During his ministry, the New International Version of the Bible became the norm in the pulpit, in place of the Authorised (King James) Version, which had been *de rigeur* until then. To select one series above others is invidious, but the congregation's response to Mr. Prime's preaching through First Corinthians, on Sunday mornings from Easter 1984 to Easter 1985, was a turning point in the life of the church. People took to heart particularly 'Working Together' (chapters 1–3), 'Responsibility for Each Other' (chapters 8 and 9) and 'Using Spiritual Gifts' (chapters 12–14). Students delayed their return home at the end of term, so as not to miss the last in the series before the summer break, and regular attenders volunteered to become involved in church activities in a new way. Indeed, it might be said that this 'hearing' of a familiar book, through the detailed expository preaching of it, equipped the church for what turned out to be a five year Vacancy soon afterward.

The Search Committee, formed when Mr Prime relinquished the pastorate in October 1987, recognised the importance of preaching by placing the public exposition of Scripture at the top of the list of qualifications which (the Committee believed) they should look for in a successor. They were therefore delighted when Rev. Peter Grainger, who had preached three times in the Chapel with great power and freedom, accepted a call and came to Edinburgh in August 1992. While the message remains the same, the most appropriate presentation of it evolves from time to time. The last decade has brought the printing of sermon outlines for distribution at the beginning of the service, then the projection of these onto screens during the preaching, and now the availability of these outlines on the Internet. A packed Church, particularly on Sunday mornings, proves that there is still hunger and appreciation for expository preaching.

How, then, might one use this book of sermon outlines? First, and above all else, by accepting the Bible as the inspired Word of God. Secondly, by using the outlines to search its contents systematically, with reverence and thoroughness. Thirdly, to apply its precepts to heart and life. There has been no occupant of the Chapel pulpit, in the two centuries of its history, be his gifts many or few, who has not bowed before the authority of Scripture and claimed a hearing for its message with a prophetic 'Thus says the Lord'. Expository preaching has moulded, and is still moulding, those who 'trust and obey'.

This book is therefore commended because it gives those who have heard the sermons another opportunity of reflecting on them, and it gives those who have not heard them the opportunity of looking in a fresh way at the passages outlined.

Ian Balfour is a lawyer in Edinburgh and is currently writing a history of Charlotte Chapel. He is the present Church Secretary.

Preparing to Preach

O ne of the questions I am most frequently asked about my role as a Pastor is, *'How long does it take you to prepare a sermon?'* Most people are surprised by my answer, *'At least ten hours and often as long as fifteen or even twenty hours.'*

The assumption seems to be that, as with any other task, the person who performs it regularly will be able to complete it quickly – and certainly much more speedily than the occasional 'amateur'.

However, while the trained preacher may have a facility with the Biblical text and languages and a familiarity with the Biblical resources that others lack, none the less the task of sermon preparation is very demanding and time-consuming.

The main reason for this is that preaching is unlike any other task, in that the pastor/preacher is entrusted with the awesome responsibility of presenting God's Word to a congregation – and to the same congregation every Sunday (often morning and evening) for many years.

Such a task, if carried out faithfully and undertaken seriously, can never be a mere mechanical process, but is something living and vital which occupies my thinking and praying (and even sleeping!) moments throughout the week – and not just the ten to twenty hours in the study.

Choosing a subject

The first task of the preacher is deciding which Biblical passage and particular subject to preach on. While the practice of preaching on unrelated topics every week was favoured by famous preachers such as C. H. Spurgeon, the expository preaching method of preaching through a Biblical book or theme has much to commend it – especially in a long-term ministry in the same church.

However, while the topic and passage for each sermon are planned beforehand, considerable thought and prayer is needed before deciding on a series and its relevance to a particular congregation. There is nothing worse than wondering, in week four of a two year series on 1 John, whether you may have made a wrong choice!

The wise pastor knows his congregation and their needs and history, so he chooses his series prayerfully and carefully, often in discussion with others leaders in the church. So, for example, I began my ministry in Charlotte Chapel with a series on the letters to the seven churches in Revelation 1–3 as a diagnostic check-list of the kind of church we were and what the Spirit was saying to this particular church at this specific point in our history.

How long should a series last? This depends partly on the topic or book that is chosen but is also determined by other factors. While many have tried to imitate the practice of Dr. Martyn Lloyd-Jones who spent several years on one New Testament Epistle, I believe that the level of Biblical literacy is so poor these days, that newcomers to the Christian faith need a broader exposure to a whole range of Scripture over a shorter period (added to which very few of us have the ability of the Doctor to sustain such long in-depth series).

It has been our practice in Charlotte Chapel to adopt a particular theme and verse for each year which is usually addressed on Sunday mornings. So, for example, our theme for 1997 was *Building on the Rock'* – a series of sermons on the Sermon on the Mount with the key verse of Matthew 7:24:

'Therefore everyone who hears these words of mine and puts them into practice is like a wise man who built his house on the rock.'

This series of thirty-four messages took the whole year (allowing for special Sundays and seasons) but most series are much shorter – for example, the series on John the Baptist, *'A Voice Crying in the Wilderness'*, which was only six sermons.

We also try to provide a balanced diet for the congregation, often having a series from the Old Testament in the morning and one from the New Testament in the evening, or an evening evangelistic series aimed at seekers, alternating with a morning teaching series directed towards Christians. In this book you will find a sample of these different kinds of series with outlines for each message in the series and the relevant Biblical passage.

So, how do I spend those hours in the study preparing to preach? There is no *'divine blueprint'* but the following is my normal practice. After preaching on Sunday, I take Monday as my day off (a personal Sabbath for rest and renewal). The one or two sermons which have occupied so much thought and effort during the previous week, and have now been discharged, are relegated from the forefront to the background of my thinking – not exactly *'deleted'* but at least placed in the *'recycle bin'*.

So on Tuesday morning I (hopefully) begin with a refreshed mind and a relaxed body – preparing to preach on the chosen passage and topic on the coming Sunday morning or evening – or both. In Charlotte Chapel, we normally have an Assistant Pastor who will preach twice a month which means that I have two Sundays each month when I am only preaching once. This allows me some latitude to do other things in those weeks – and also to hear God's Word from someone else on those Sundays. I try to avoid the preacher's syndrome of speaking elsewhere every time I have a free Sunday and to be as good a listener to others as I hope they are to me.

Groundwork

My first task is groundwork – to familiarise myself with the Biblical passage in order to make sure that I understand what it says and means. To help me do this, I read the text in several different translations ranging from the more literal through to paraphrases (we use the New International Version in Charlotte Chapel). A knowledge of the original languages (Greek and Hebrew) is useful though not essential as there are many excellent commentaries and other resources which define words and meanings.

Commentaries and other books fall into two broad categories. Some major on exegesis – explaining the meaning of the text to those who were its original recipients, often with detailed analysis of words and phrases in the original languages. Others, including books of sermons, focus on application – trying to understand the relevance of the text for us today. Many included both categories but are usually stronger on one than the other.

As I read these books, I make rough notes on anything useful, noting any useful sentences or sections that might be worth quoting directly (if I do so, I always acknowledge the source –out of courtesy and honesty, and also hopefully to encourage others to buy and read the book).

In the introduction to each series in this book, I have listed a few of the books that we found particularly useful. D. A. Carson's

New Testament Commentary Survey (IVP:1993) is a useful resource which summarises the strengths and weaknesses of commentaries for the New Testament. And, although he preached over a century ago, I find that Spurgeon's sermons usually shed fresh light on any given passage.

Building-work

After groundwork, comes building-work – an attempt to put the material into some semblance of order. Although I accept that some hearers and speakers favour a holistic approach to preaching and learning – describing a broad theme and then coming at it from different angles – I am not one of them. I am a linear progressive thinker and preacher and so I find it helpful to analyse the structure of the passage or theme and divide it into several major points (usually anything from two to four or five depending on the topic).

As you will see from the outlines in this book, I try to make these as memorable as possible – using alliteration or balanced phrases, so long as they are not forced. This will also be determined by the type of passage – narrative is very different from discourse, parable from proverb, or Gospel from Epistle. I sometimes struggle to find a good structure and find that sleeping on it is often beneficial.

Application

Perhaps the hardest part of all is application and, rather than spending thirty minutes on explanation and then only the last five minutes on application, I try to include the application as I go along with each major point. However, I usually attempt to isolate one major point which summarises the theme of the passage and which the hearer can take away.

I find that a suitable **title** for the sermon can help to do this. Again, I know that some people, such as Dr Martyn Lloyd Jones did not favour titles, but it is surely significant that the editors of his sermons have given titles to each of them! The title can also arouse interest if it is advertised ahead of time – depending on the choice. A church I visited recently had an attractive leaflet with the sermon topics, but the title for Luke 8:40–48 was *'Woman with haemorrhage'!* Something more imaginative such as *'Living with long-term illness'* or *'Hoping for healing'* might have attracted a wider audience!

Another aid to focusing on the theme is the **opening section** of the sermon. Working on the well-known premise *'If you don't strike oil in the first five minutes, stop boring!'*, I choose with care an opening illustration to catch the listener's attention. This can be drawn from personal experience or from the current news or some topical issue which engages with the hearers.

For example, on one occasion, I was due to speak on the attitude of Jesus to the Sabbath and in that very week I read in the newspaper that the Chief Rabbi in Israel had announced that throwing snowballs on the Sabbath was against the Mosaic law (unless those you threw them at gave their permission!) It made an excellent introduction to Sunday's topic!

Finally, I try to drive the main point home with a **concluding illustration** – sometimes returning to the one with which I began or even adding some further details. A sample sermon is included at the back of this book.

You will see from this sermon that I prepare very full notes from which to preach. When I began preaching in my teens, I prided myself on three points written on the back of an old envelope. As I have got older (and wiser?!) I find that writing out in full helps me to think through what I want to say. I then familiarise myself with the material and use the notes as a prop rather than reading verbatim from them.

Computers

A word about computers which I believe are a brilliant resource for the preacher. First of all, the material in the sermon can be edited and moved around quite readily and easily. Then there are many resources available on computer including commentaries, concordances, maps and lexicons and many Bible versions which can be cut and pasted into the text of the sermon.

Finally, there is the Internet, which has an amazing store of useful information. For example, I was recently preaching on the theme of *'Finishing Well'* and wanted to use the famous story of the marathon runner Jim Peters who collapsed just before the finishing line. A simple search on the internet gave all the details of time and place and even photographs! Incidentally, I believe that illustrations gain much greater credibility with the listeners if they are cited accurately.

The sermon outlines included in this book are included in the church bulletin which people receive as they enter the church, and have proved to be popular and useful to most people. One disadvantage with this is that people can see what is coming and so any sense of surprise or anticipation is lost.

One way around this is to put the outline on a screen with overhead transparencies or via a computer. In Charlotte Chapel we now use PowerPoint presentation as an aid to the sermon in place of the written outline, and these can be downloaded from our website (www.charlottechapel.org).

Preaching – in its style and structure as well as its preparation – is very personal, and I am very aware of this fact as I offer these observations and the series and outlines which follow. However, if an idea for a series or a title for a sermon, or an approach to a passage can be of some help to a fellow preacher, then I hope this book will be worthwhile. While most of these outlines are my own, I am grateful to colleagues who have shared in these sermon series with me and have allowed their outlines to be included in this book – in particular, our former Assistant Pastor, Rev. John Smuts, and my predecessor, Rev. Derek Prime.

Perhaps the greatest beneficiary of the sermon is the preacher himself, for only the message which is first of all addressed and applied to me will carry any real authenticity when preached to others. In order for this to happen, both preacher and hearers need the illumination and help of the Holy Spirit. Without that divine empowering, the most thorough of preparation and most professional of presentation will prove to be mere words. With the Holy Spirit's help, the words of the poorest of preachers can become the very words of God.

For those who may be interested in the spoken sermons behind the outlines in this book, most of them are available on tape from:

The Tape Ministry, Charlotte Baptist Chapel, West Rose Street, EDINBURGH EH2 4AZ

1

A Spiritual Check-up
(Revelation 1–3)

One of the advantages of ministering in a church over a long period, is that the pastor/teacher chooses (with the help of the Holy Spirit) to preach from a book or theme which is of particular relevance to the needs or condition of the church and congregation. However, when you first arrive in a church, you are largely unaware of these issues and thus choosing what to preach about is that much more difficult.

Taking this approach, I began my ministry in Charlotte Chapel by preaching from the opening chapters of the last book in the Bible – the Book of Revelation. While some expositors see the seven churches that are addressed as successive stages in Christian history (with the present state always being that of Laodicea, the last church), others see them as a cross-section of the different kinds and states of local churches at any time in history.

With this in mind, we considered together 'what the Spirit is saying' – not only to the churches, but to our local church in particular, and asked and attempted to answer the key question: 'Which of the seven churches in Revelation are we most like in Charlotte Chapel? What is the Spirit saying to us and how should we respond?'

There is an abundance of material on the Book of Revelation in general and the letters to the churches in particular (describing the historical setting and background of each church which is the key to the messages addressed to them) and a few are listed here.

The Tyndale New Testament Commentary on *Revelation* by Leon Morris (IVP, 1969) gives a good, though brief, commentary on the text. 'The Bible Speaks Today' on *Revelation* by Michael Wilcox (IVP, 1975) has additional application for the preacher. The commentary by Philip Edgcumbe Hughes (IVP & Eerdmans, 1990) includes his own translation and focuses on how the book's symbolism is drawn from and shaped by the Old Testament. William Hendriksen's *More than Conquerors* (1940 – British Edition, Tyndale Press, 1962) has become a classical amillennial interpretation of the Book of Revelation.

William Barclay's *Daily Study Bible* (The Saint Andrew Press, 1959) has helpful background material. For a guided tour through the book of Revelation, see Richard Bewes *The Lamb Wins*, (Christian Focus, 2000)

On the letters to the seven churches in particular, Theodore H. Epp's *Christ Speaks to the Church* (Good News Broadcasting, 1960) and (more recently) Mike Breen's *The Body Beautiful* (Monarch, 1997) have useful material for the preacher.

Finally, John Stott's *What Christ Thinks of the Church* (Angus Hudson Ltd/Three's Company, 1990) contains not only helpful text and application but also beautiful colour pictures of the ancient sites of the seven churches which can still be seen and visited today.

At the end of this book is a sample sermon – full notes of the message on EPHESUS – FIRST LOVE FORSAKEN (Revelation 2: 1–7)

1. What John saw
(Revelation 1:9–20)

What is now' – a **vision of Jesus** :

1. **He is the Lord of Glory (verses 13–17a)**

   • his **humanity** – *'like a son of man'*

   • his **divinity** – the Son of God

John's reaction – *'I fell at his feet as though dead'*

2. **He is the Lord of life and death (verses 17b–18)**

   • his **death** – *'I was dead'*

   • his **resurrection** – *'I am alive for ever and ever'*

The Lord's response – his touch and his word – *'do not be afraid'*

3. **He is the Lord of his Church (verses 19–20)**

   • his **control** – he holds the *'seven stars'*

   • his **activity** – he walks *'among the lampstands'*

John's responsibility – *'write......'*

Our position
   • *'in Patmos'* – we **suffer**
   • *'in the Spirit'* – we **reign**

2. Ephesus – first love forsaken
(Revelation 2:1–7)

Ephesus – a leading **city** and a leading **church** (Acts 19–20)

A **message from the Lord** who **sees and knows** (verse 2)

1. **Commendation (verses 2–3, 6)**
   Two reasons for praise

   • **determination** in the face of **hardship** (Acts 14:21–22)

   • **discrimination** in the face of **heresy** (Acts 20:26–31)

2. **Criticism (verse 4)**
   One matter of supreme importance

   • great love **understood** (see Ephesians and 1 John)

   • first love **abandoned** (Jeremiah 2:2, 32)

3. **Correction (verse 5a)**
   Three steps that must be taken

   • **remember** (Luke 15:17)

   • **repent** (Luke 15:18–20)

   • **repeat**

A **warning** (verse 5b) and a **promise** (verse 7b)

3. Smyrna – death and life
(Revelation 2:8–11)

The **difficult situation** the church faced
- intense pressure
- abject poverty
- unjustified slander
- approaching persecution

Yet a **message of hope** from the risen Lord Jesus

1. The CITY which died and lived
- out of destruction
- a new and prosperous city

2. The LORD who died and lives
JESUS
- the First
- the Last

3. The CHRISTIANS who die and live
What the Lord **says to his faithful followers**
- *'I know'* – about your **present situation**

- *'Do not be afraid'* – about **future persecution**
  - it will be **used for testing**
  - it will be **limited in duration**

- *'Be faithful'*
  - *'to the point of death'*
  - *'a crown of life'*

4. Pergamum – living where Satan has his throne
(Revelation 2:12–17)

1.   **Satan's seat**
Pergamum – a centre for

- the worship of the Greek gods

- the worship of 'Asclepios the Saviour'

- the worship of Caesar

2.   **Satan's strategy**

- **outright opposition** – which did not succeed

- **subtle seduction** – which was more successful
  - idolatry and
  - immorality

3. **The Lord's power**
The Lord's sword
   - the symbol of real power

   - used against those who will not repent

4. **The Lord's promise**

Future blessings for *'those who overcome'*
- *'hidden manna'* (see John 6:30–35)

- *'a white stone with a new name'*

5. Thyatira – no compromise!
(Revelation 2:18–29)

Three words about the **city** – and the **church**

1. Industry

- the **city** : a hive of **commercial activity**

- the **church** – **active and devoted service to God**

2. Vulnerability

- the **city** – impossible to **defend**

- the **church** – open to **attack**
    - **religious compromise** through
    - **business practices** leading to
    - **immorality** and **idolatry**

3. Deity

The Son of God *'who searches hearts and minds'*
- **repent** – or you will be **judged**

- **be obedient** – and you will be **blessed**
    - **authority** over the nations

    - **intimacy** with the risen Christ

'Hold on to what you have' – *'until I come'.*

7. The heart of the matter
(Matthew 5:8)

A connection between the heart and the eyes

1. **The requirement – *'pure in heart'***
The **meaning**
   - *'pure'* = not just about morality,
     but rather **integrity**
   - *'the heart'* = not just the emotions,
     but the **whole person**

   The *'heart problem'*
   - **depravity** – not purity (Romans 7:14–24)
   - **deception** – not honesty (Matthew 15:1–20)

   The **only** *'cure'* – Psalm 51:10; Romans 7:25

2. **The reward – *'they will see God'***
Present – *'by faith'* (Hebrews 11:27)
   - in creation (Psalm 19:1–6)
   - in the Scriptures (Psalm 19:7–11)
   - in every experience (Romans 8:28)
   - in JESUS (2 Corinthians 4:6)

   Future – *'face to face'*
   - an encouragement (1 Corinthians 13:12)
   - an incentive (1 John 3:1–3)

8. Like Father, like son
(Matthew 5:9)

Peacemaking :characteristic of **the Father** – then of **his children**

1.   **'Like Father, like Son'**

Peace = harmony, well–being (not just the absence of war)

- the **problem** of peace (Genesis 3)

- the **process** of peace
    initiated – by God (2 Corinthians 5:18–19)
    promised – by the prophets (Isaiah 9:1–7)
    inaugurated – by Jesus (Luke 2:14; 29–32)

- the **price** of peace (Colossians 1:19–22)

- the **product** of peace – **reconciliation**
    with **God**   (Romans 5:1)
    with **others**   (Ephesians 2:11–22)

2.   **'Like father, like son'**

Peacemaking – a character trait **inherited from the Father**

- the **proclamation** of peace (Romans 10:14–15)

- the **pursuit** of peace
    with fellow–Christians (5:23–24; 1 Peter 3:8–11)
    with all people (Romans 12:17–21; Matthew 5:43–48)

- the **prospect** of peace (Isaiah 11:6–9; Romans 16:20)

9. The blessing of persecution
(Matthew 5:10–12)

Persecution – the natural outcome of living out the other Beatitudes.

Jesus **highlights**

1. **The reality of persecution**

   Persecution
   - takes **different forms** – *'slaughter and slander'*
   - is **inevitable** for every Christian – expect it!

   Be encouraged – it is part of our normal Christian experience

2. **The reason for persecution**

   - **false** reason – living in the **wrong** manner (1 Peter 4:15)
   - **true** reason – living in a **Christlike** manner (vv. 10–11)

   Identifying with Jesus = being treated as he was (John 15:18–20)

   Be challenged – if we never face **any** opposition, are we truly seeking to live like Christ? (2 Timothy 3:12)

3. **The response to persecution**

   Don't retaliate or be resentful – instead **rejoice and be glad** (v. 12), because **persecution reminds us of**

   - **who we are** – our place in the kingdom (v. 10)
   - **what lies ahead** – our reward in heaven (v. 12)

   Be confident – in Christ's power (John 16:33)

10. The salt of the earth
(Matthew 5:13)

Salt and light – the function of the Christian in society (vv.13–16)
Two characteristics of salt:

1. **Distinctiveness**
   The Christian is **identifiable by**

   - **character displayed**
            described by Jesus – vv. 3–9
            produced by the Spirit – Galatians 5:22–23

   - **reaction aroused**
        persecution – vv. 10–12
        like the Master – John 15:18–22; (Luke 14:25–34)

   Question – am I **different?**

2. **Effectiveness**
   Two emphases:
   - **preservation** – in a **sick** society (negative)
        small
        unobtrusive

   - **flavouring** – in a **sad** society (positive)
        'life to the full' (John 10:10)
        speech (Colossians 4:6)

   Question – am I **effective?**

The Great Danger :
   - **compromise with the world,** which makes me
   - **useless to God** (compare the Pharisees – see 8:12)

11. The light of the world
(Matthew 5:14–16)

The background – **light in darkness** (Genesis 1:1–3)

Three themes about *'the light of the world'*

1. **Light derived**
    'God is light' (1 John 1:5)
    *   **Jesus** – *'the light of the world'* (John 8:12, 9:5)
    *   **disciples** – *'sons of light'* (John 12:36)
    'Live as children of light' (Ephesians 5:8–21; 4:17–32)

2. **Light displayed**
    Light must **function naturally**
    *   *'a city on a hill'* – it **cannot** be hidden
    *   *'a lamp under a bowl'* – it **should** not be hidden
    The **function of God's people** (1 Peter 2:9–12; Rev. 2:5)

3. **Light described**
    The **demonstration of light:**
    *   **good deeds** (Ephesians 2:8–10)
    *   **praise** to *'your Father in heaven'* (contrast 6:1–34)
        supernatural – like the Father
        'of the world' – *'in heaven'*
    'Treasure in jars of clay' (2 Corinthians 4:6–7)

12. Living in the kingdom
(Matthew 5:17–20)

The issue – **what law** do the citizens of the *'kingdom of heaven'* live under?

Three essential requirements for *'living in the kingdom'*

1. **The *'law'* that must be fulfilled (vv. 17–18)**
   Jesus **fulfils** *'the Law and the Prophets'*
   - the **Prophets** – fulfilled in the details of his life
     (e.g. 1:22–23; 2:6, Isaiah 7:14; Jeremiah 31:15, etc.)
   - the **Law** – fulfilled in
       - his birth   (Galatians 4:4)
       - his baptism   (3:14–15)
       - his death   (Galatians 3:13)
   Fulfilled in **the Christian** (Romans 8:1–4)

2. **The *'commandments'* that must be obeyed (v. 19)**
   The commands of Jesus must be
   - practised (7:24)
   - taught (28:18–20)
   Obedience – the key to living in the kingdom

3. **The *' righteousness'* that must be exceeded (v. 20)**
   Two kinds of *'righteousness'*
   - practised **by the Pharisees and teachers of the law**
     (see 23)
       - superficial
       - human effort
       - glory to self (6:2, 5, 16)
   - demanded **by Jesus** (see 5:21ff)
       - from the heart (Jeremiah 31:33)
       - by the Spirit (Galatians 5:22–25)
       - glory to God (v. 16)

13. The meaning of murder
(Matthew 5:21–26)

Three kinds of murder

1. **Murder by action**
    'Do not murder' – a contrast between
    •   what is **written** – the Law of Moses (Exodus 20:13)
    •   what is **said** – human tradition (15:7–9)
    'But I tell you..' – the **authority of Jesus** (7:28–29)

2. **Murder by anger**
    The **seriousness of anger**
    •   an **equal crime** with murder
    •   an **equal punishment** as murder
    A *'heart–problem'* (Mark 7:20–23) which **produces other
    symptoms** (e.g. Genesis 4:1–16 – see 1 John 3:11–15)

3. **Murder by word**
    The problem of **verbal abuse**
    •   *'Raca'* – an attack on the **head**
    •   *'Fool'* – an attack on the **heart**
    Danger – a severe warning (12:36–37)

The solution – reconciliation must be sought
    •   **immediately** – the brother in the church
                    before worship (Psalm 66:18)
    •   **urgently** – the adversary in the court
                    before it is too late (1 Samuel 15:22–29)

14. Radical teaching on adultery
(Matthew 5:27–30)

The teaching of Jesus is **radical**
— different, revolutionary (see 7:28–29)
— to the heart (*'root'*) of the matter (Mark 7:18–23)

1.   **A radical definition of the nature of adultery (vv. 27–28)**

A **contrast** between
• what is **'heard'**
    — the law – Exodus 20:14 (Deuteronomy 5:18)
    — the act only (though see Exodus 20:17)
• what Jesus **'says'**
    — looking lustfully
    — adultery *'in the heart'*

The need for **'a pure heart'** (Psalm 51:10; 5:3–10)

2.   **A radical solution for the problem of adultery (vv. 29–30)**

How to **avoid being ensnared**
• **personal responsibility**
    — *'if your eye....'*
    — *'if your hand...'*
• **painful surgery**
    — *'put to death....'* (Colossians 3:5–6)
    — *'do not think about...'* (Romans 13:12–14)

Eternal consequences (10:26–28; 1 Corinthians 9:26–27)

15. Marriage matters
(Matthew 5:31–32)

The focus – prevention not cure

The key – understanding marriage (Genesis 2:18–25; Ephesians 5:31–33)

1.   **The proper context of divorce**

   The teaching of Jesus **in relation to**
   - lust and adultery (vv. 27–30)
   - the law of Moses (Deuteronomy 24:1–4)
   - God's creation (19:3–12; Mark 10:1–12;)

2.   **The permissible condition for divorce**

   'Marital unfaithfulness'
   - not in Mark (10:11–12) or Luke (16:18)
   - not *'adultery'* (vv. 27–28)
   - not commanded but allowed (Mark 10:3–4)

3.   **The possible consequence from divorce**

   How God views **those involved**
   - *'commits adultery'* (19:9)
   - *'caused to commit adultery'*
   - free to remarry?

The divine husband woos his unfaithful wife (Hosea 2:14–23)

16. Nothing but the truth
(Matthew 5:33–37)

The context:the swearing of oaths

1.   **What the Law of Moses said about oaths**

     Practised between
     •   people (e.g. Genesis 21:22–24; 24:3; 25; 33)
     •   God and people (Genesis 22:16–18; Heb. 6:13–20)
     Sanctioned by God – see Leviticus 19:12; Numbers 30:2;
     Deuteronomy 23:21

2.   **What the Pharisees said about oaths**

     A **false interpretation** of God's law
     •   abusing words (see 23:16–22)
     •   excluding God (vv. 34–35; Exodus 20:7)
     The result: deceitfulness and untrustworthiness

3.   **What Jesus said about oaths**

     They should **not be necessary**
     •   your word is enough (v. 37; James 5:12)
     •   anything more is
          — *'from the evil'*? (12:33–37)
          — *'from the evil one'*? (6:13; John 8:43–45)
     An **example to follow:** 1 Peter 2:21–23

17. The mind of Christ
(Matthew 5:38–42)

Some of the **best known** yet **most misinterpreted** words of Jesus

1. **Understanding the teaching of Jesus in context**

   The background – the Law of Moses (Leviticus 24:17–21)
   • limited (not excessive) punishment
   • judicial (not personal) administration (Rom. 12:17 – 13:7)
   Abused by the Pharisees, but **addressed to disciples** (vv. 1–20)

2. **Applying the words of Jesus in principle**

   Not new laws but **great principles**, focusing on rights
   • dignity (John 18:22–23)
   • security (Exodus 22:26–27)
   • autonomy (Matthew 27:32)
   • property (Mark 12:41–44)
   Asserted by the world **but willingly abandoned by disciples** who are

3. **Following the example of Jesus in practice**

   The way of Jesus is **the way of the cross**
   • suffering unjustly (1 Peter 2:20–25)
   • denying self (Matthew 16:24–26)
   • living by the Spirit (Galatians 5:16–26)
   Secure in God's love in Christ – Romans 8:28–39

18.   Two kinds of love
(Matthew 5:43–48)

The contrast between the love that Jesus demands of his disciples and that of the rest of society.

1.   Human love – *'love those who love you'*

Such love is seen
- among the *'pagans'*
- even among *'tax–collectors'*
- (sadly) among the Jews (Leviticus 19:18)
  — *'love your neighbour'* (but see Luke 10:25–37)
  — *'hate your enemy'* (but see Exodus 23:4–5)

Jesus demands **love of a different kind**

2.   Divine love – *'love those who hate you'*

Such love is seen
- in the Father (Jonah 4:10–11)
- in the Son (John 4:1–42; Luke 23:34)
- in the *'sons'* (1 John 4:7–8; Acts 7:60)

The goal – *'perfection'* (v. 48; 1 John 4:16–18)

19. Two kinds of giving
(Matthew 6:1–4)

'Acts of righteousness' – giving (vv. 2–4), praying (vv. 5–14) and fasting (vv. 16–18).

The **contrast with current religious practice** – *'do not be like them'*

1.   **'Showy' giving (v. 2)**

The **'act'** of giving
- *'theatre'* (v. 1)
- *'hypocrites'* (vv. 5, 16)
- *'trumpets'* (v. 2)
- *'audience'* (vv. 1–2)

The **'reward'** – *'applause'* – and **nothing more**

2.   **'Secret' giving (vv. 3–4)**

A different **motive** (compare 5:16)
- done *'in secret'*
- forgotten by the giver (25:31–46)
- seen by *'your Father'* (6:10)

The **'reward'** – the **Father's approval** – now and in eternity

20. When you pray
(Matthew 6:5–8)

'Be careful!' (v. 1)

Two problems *'when you pray'*

1.   **The problem of hypocrisy (vv. 5–6)**

      'Pray–acting' – a problem for the **Jews**
- **audience**
  'in the synagogues'
  'on the street corners'
- **applause**
  'received their reward'
  'in full'

The remedy – *'your Father **sees**'*
- **secrecy** – from others
- **intimacy** – with God

2.   **The problem of verbosity (vv. 7–8)**

  'Babbling' – a problem for the **Gentiles** (e.g. 1 Kings 18:25–39)
- irrational
- repetitive
- lengthy

The remedy – *'your Father **knows**'*
- *'what you need'* (vv. 28–32)
- *'before you ask him'* (Isaiah 65:24)

21. Radical teaching on prayer
(Matthew 6:9)

The **contrast** – *'do not be like them'* (vv. 5 & 8)

1. **The pattern for how we should pray**
   'This, then, is how you should pray'

   Words – and **meaning** (compare Luke 11:2–4)
   - concerns **first** about **God**
     'your name' (v. 9)
     'your kingdom' (v. 10a)
     'your will' (v. 10b)

   - concerns **then** about **self**
     'give us...' (v. 11)
     'forgive us...' (v. 12)
     'deliver us...' (v. 13)

2. **The person to whom we should pray**
   'Our Father in heaven'

   - **'Father'**
     personal – willing to help
     intimate – confidence

   - **'in heaven'**
     powerful – able to help
     transcendent – reverence

   'Our' – adopted into God's family through Jesus (Gal. 3:26 – 4:7)

3. **The priority for which we should pray**

   'Hallowed be your name'
   The Father's character to be **known and reverenced**:
   - in the world (v. 10)
   - in our lives (1 Peter 1:14–17)

22. 'Give us today our daily bread'
(Matthew 6:11)

'Down to earth' from vv. 9–10.

Four themes:

1.　*'Bread'* – Necessity

　　Our **needs** – not our **greeds**
　　　　•　　the prayer of **Agur** (Proverbs 30:8–9)
　　　　•　　the warning of **Paul** (1 Timothy 6:6–10)
　　In **accordance with God's will** (v. 10)

2.　*'Us'* – Generosity

　　Family character
　　　　•　　a generous **Father** (7:11)
　　　　•　　his generous **children** (Acts 2:44–45)
　　Dead faith? (James 2:14–17)

3.　*'Today'* & *'daily'* – Dependency

　　Enough for *'each day'* (Luke 11:3)
　　　　•　　the danger of **ignoring God** (Luke 12:15–21)
　　　　•　　the danger of **forgetting God** (Deut. 6:10–12)
　　Give thanks to the Giver (Matthew 26:26)

4.　*'Give'* – Intimacy

　　Do not
　　　　•　　*'babble'* – your Father **knows** (vv. 7–8)
　　　　•　　*'worry'* – your Father **cares** (vv. 25–34)
　　But your Father **wants you to ask** (7:7–11)

23. The forgiving father
(Matthew 6:12, 14–15)

'Forgive us our debts, as we also have forgiven our debtors' – **understanding what Jesus meant**.

1.   A prayer of the forgiven

Forgiveness **begins with God:**
- our *'debt'* (18:24) (or *'sin'/ 'trespass'* – Luke 11:4)
- God's **initiative** (Romans 5:6–11)

So, the Lord's Prayer is *'The Children's Prayer'* (see Luke 15:21–24)

2.   A prayer of the forgiving

Forgiveness **flows from God**
- we **should** forgive others – far less to forgive (18:28)
- we **must** forgive others – *'from the heart'* (18:35)

Or we **cut ourselves off from God's love** (1 John 4:20)

3.   A prayer for forgiveness

My **continuing need** – *'daily bread'* (v.11) **and** daily forgiveness (v.12)
- an awareness of **my great sin**
- an awareness of **God's great love**

The result – my **continuing forgiveness** (18:21–22; Col. 3:13)

24. A prayer for protection
(Matthew 6:13)

The final petition – an **antidote against complacency**

Three implications for the Christian

1.   **I face a formidable enemy**

'The evil one' who **tempts people to sin:**
   • his **success** – Genesis 3:1–24
   • his **failure** – Matthew 4:1–11
His **strategies** – 1 Peter 5:8; 2 Corinthians 11:14 (and 2:11)

2.   **I am a vulnerable target**

The **devil's attacks:**
   • through his *'children'* (John 8:44)
   • against **Jesus** and against **his followers** John 15:18–25)
The **weakness of the sinful nature** (Romans 7:14–24)

3.   **I have a dependable Father**

Promised protection *'from the evil one'* (John 17:15)
   • **a way out** from the temptation (1 Corinthians 10:13)
   • **a purpose** in the trial (2 Cor. 12:7–10; James 1:2–3)
Future assurance– *'the test'* (Revelation 3:10; 2 Timothy 4:18)

The Doxology –
'For yours is the kingdom and the power and the glory for ever. Amen.'

25. When you fast
(Matthew 6:16–18)

A third *'act of righteousness'* (6:1) for the disciple of Jesus (9:14–15).

1.   **What?**
Fasting is the
   • voluntary
   • abstinence
   • from something legitimate (or essential)
   • for a limited period
   • for a specific purpose

2.   **When?**
Two kinds of fasts
   • set fasts for all (Leviticus 16:29–34)
   • personal fasts for the individual (Nehemiah 1:4)
The Pharisees – *'twice weekly'* (Luke 18:12)

3.   **Why?**
Seeking God at **times of particular need** (with prayer)
   • sorrow for sin & seeking mercy (1 Samuel 7:6; Joel 2:12–14)
   • lamentation over bad news (2 Samuel 1:12)
   • facing a crisis & seeking help (2 Samuel 12:16)
   • seeking direction & taking decisions (Acts 13:2–3; 14:23)

4.   **How?**
Two ways of fasting
   • hypocritically (v. 16)
   • secretly (vv. 17–18)
Two rewards (v. 16 & 18)

26. An antidote for anxiety
(Matthew 6:25–34)

A negative and positive **remedy for the problem of worry**

1. **A negative habit to avoid –**
    'don't worry' (vv. 25–32, 34) because

    •   worry is **pointless** – a lesson for **everyone**
         height or length of life (v. 27)
         tomorrow's troubles (v. 34)

    •   worry is **faithless** – a lesson for **disciples**
         birds – life – food (v. 26)
         flowers – the body – clothing (vv. 28–30)

    A **heavenly Father** – or a *'pagan'* outlook? (vv. 31–32)

2. **A positive goal to pursue –**
    'seek first' (v. 33) – *'worry'* about

    •   God's **kingdom**
    •   God's **righteousness**
Then *'all these things will be given you as well'* (see 6:9–11)

27. A matter of judgement
(Matthew 7:1–6)

Jesus calls for **balanced judgement in our attitude to others**

1.   Seeing *'Specks of sawdust'* (vv. 1–5) –
     the danger of judging others **too critically**

   the **symptoms:**
   * **selectivity**
     — on the faults of others (not my own)
     — on the small faults of others (not my large ones)
   *   **severity**
     — condemnation
     — taking on the role of God (James 4:11–12)

   the **antidote:**
   * **priority** – *'first....'* (James 1:22–25)
   * **consequence** – *'then....'* (Matthew 18:15–17)

2.   Seeing *'Dogs and pigs'* (v. 6) –
     the danger of judging others **too indiscriminately**

           'what is sacred' (Exodus 29:33–34)
           'pearls' (13:45–46)

   should **not be given** to
           'dogs' (Psalm 22:16–20)
           'pigs' (Leviticus 11:7–8)

   The **abuse** of the **message** and the **messenger** –
   see 10:11– 33; Acts 18:5–6; Luke 23:8–9

28. Receiving – and giving
(Matthew 7:7–12)

The **key to understanding** these verses – the **context**.

1.   **Receiving – from God (vv. 7–11)**

Three characteristics of **prayer**
- **dependence** – my need for God's help
  — character (5:2–16)
  — behaviour (5:17– 7:6)
- **persistence** (see Luke 15:5–10, 18:1–8)
  — wholehearted (Jeremiah 29:13)
  — despite the cost (Genesis 32:22–32)
- **assurance** – a contrast between
  — *'evil'* fathers, and
  — your *'Father in heaven.'*

The promise – *'good gifts'* (Luke 11:13)

2.   **Giving – to others (v. 12)**

'So....' – love your neighbour as yourself (Mark 12:28–31)
- **security** – in the Father's love
- **ability** – in the Spirit's power

'The Law and the Prophets': fulfilled by **Jesus** (5:17) **and his disciples**

29. Are you on the right road?
(Matthew 7:13–14)

More radical teaching from Jesus – **the great divide**

1.   **Two Gates**

- wide
- narrow

2.   **Two Groups**

- many
- few

3.   **Two Destinations**

- destruction
- life

At the 'cross–roads'

30. The danger of deception
(Matthew 7:15–20)

'Watch out!' – a **strong warning** to **think carefully**

1. **Description (v. 15)**
   The **disguise he adopts** (2 Corinthians 11:13–15)
   - he **looks** like a sheep
   - he **sounds** like a sheep

   The **damage he inflicts**
   - diversion (Acts 13:6–8; Galatians 1:6–8, 5:7)
   - division (1 Corinthians 1:10–17)
   - destruction (Acts 20:28–31)

2. **Discrimination (vv. 16–18, 20)**
   The *'fruit'* **test**
   - the **message he speaks** (Luke 6:43–45)
   - the **life he leads** (2 Peter 2)

3. **Destination (v. 19)**
   God is not deceived (Galatians 5:7–8)
   - certain judgement (v. 23)
   - sober warning – which way? (vv. 13–14)

31. Final warning!
(Matthew 7:24–29)

The **increasing gravity** of the message – a final warning.

1.   **The man who was wise (vv. 24–25)**

He built his house **on the rock** (Luke 6:48)
- the storm struck
- the house **stood firm**

Hearing the words of Jesus and **putting them into practice**

2.   **The man who was foolish (vv. 26–27)**

He built his house **on the sand** (Luke 6:49)
- the storm struck
- the house **collapsed**

Hearing the words of Jesus and **not putting them into practice**

3.   **The man who is God (vv. 28–29)**

JESUS – the amazing teacher **or**
- **the Lord** who must be **obeyed** (vv. 21 & 24)
- **the Judge** who will **decide** (vv. 22–23)

Building on the **rock** – or **sand?**

3

Encounters with Jesus

An interesting (and important) exercise for the preacher is to check which parts and books of the Bible he preaches on most frequently and which more rarely. Do I major on the New Testament at the expense of the Old Testament, on Psalms rather than prophets, on the Epistles at the expense of the Gospels?

It is surely surprising how few gospel messages are drawn from the Gospels. I believe that the four Gospels are a rich resource of evangelistic material from which we can engage with post-modern people who relate to narrative more than discourse, and to the theme of faith as a journey of personal experience rather than a set of doctrines which must be believed (this is not to neglect the latter at the expense of the former).

With this in mind, we ran a series entitled *'Encounters with Je-sus'* featuring different individuals who met Jesus in person and whose stories are described in the Gospels. The series ran from the January to April and followed a chronological theme beginning with Simeon in the Temple and ending with the resurrection accounts and the conversion of Saul of Tarsus (straying into the Book of Acts). These can be reduced to the right number depending on the number of weeks from Christmas to Easter.

During the series we featured interviews with different people whose lives matched (where possible) the person in the encounter with Jesus – for example, a person who came to faith late in life (as with Simeon) or a younger man (the rich young ruler), and so on. We also carefully chose special music which linked with the theme. Although the series was designed with the seeker in mind, it also addressed those who had already encountered Jesus and their (continuing) journey of faith.

Close Encounters by Melvin Tinker and *Characters Around the*

Cross and *Characters Around the Cradle* by Tom Houston (Christian Focus) all touch on these themes. Any good standard commentary on a Gospel will give the necessary background.

1. The end of all my searching
(Luke 2:21–35)

SIMEON – *'a righteous and devout man'* (v. 25)

1. Waiting in hope

- for the consolation of Israel (v. 25   see Isaiah 40:1–5)

- for the fulfilment of God's promise (v. 26)

Are you **still waiting?**

2. Finding in Jesus

- salvation for sinners (vv. 30–32)

- *'a sign that will be spoken against'* (vv. 34–35)

Are you **still searching?**

3. Departing in peace

- prepared to leave

- resurrection *'rising'* (see 1 Corinthians 15:12–58)

Are you *'ready to depart?'* (Philippians 1:23; 2 Timothy 4:6–8)

2. A voice of one calling in the desert
(John 1:19–34)

The role of **JOHN THE BAPTIST**

1. Preparation for Jesus

See Isaiah 40:1–5

- repentance

- baptism   (Acts 2:38)

2. Identification of Jesus as

- the **Lamb** of God – **SAVIOUR**

  (his **death** – Isaiah 53)

- the **Son** of God – **LORD**

  (his **resurrection** – Acts 2:24–36)

Is he your Saviour and Lord?

3. The rock-maker
(John 1:35–42)

SIMON PETER – two important elements in his encounter with Jesus

1.   **What he is –**

   *'You **are** Simon, son of John'*

   John 16:7–9: the work of the Holy Spirit

2.   **What he will be –**

   *'You **will be** called Cephas'*

   The ***'rock–making*** ' **process** :

   - Luke 22:31–34

   - Luke 22:54–62

   - John 21:15–19

Who are you?

What will you become?

4. Heaven open
(John 1:43–51)

NATHANAEL – responding to Jesus

1. Prejudice

'Nazareth! Can anything good come from there?' (v. 46)

- the **answer** – 'Come and see'

- Jesus ' knows' Nathanael

2. Profession

'Rabbi, you are the Son of God; you are the King of Israel' (v. 49)

- **who** Jesus is

- **why** Jesus came

3. Promise

'You shall see heaven open' (v. 51)

- the **background** – Jacob (Genesis 28:12)

- the **fulfilment** – Mark 15:33–39

The **final fulfilment** :Matthew 26:64. – heaven **open** – and **closed**

5. Able and willing
(Mark 1:40–45)

THE LEPER – a **needy person** meets with **someone who can help him**

1. **The Leper : Desperation**

   The **effects** of his leprosy :

   - personal
   - social
   - religious

   Romans 3:23   – a **far greater problem**
   Romans 6:23   – a **far worse prognosis**

2. **Jesus : Compassion**

   - willingness   (John 3:16)
   - ability   (Hebrews 7:25)

   'Don't tell...but show...'

Conclusion

- our desperate need is met by

- God's wonderful compassion in Jesus

The **only problem – unwillingness** (Matthew 23:37)

6. The kind of person Jesus calls
(Luke 5:7–32)

LEVI – five facts about his encounter with Jesus

1. **Call**   *'Follow me'* (v. 27)

    •   personal

    •   as he was

2. **Commitment**
    'Levi got up, left everything and followed him' (v. 28)

    •   the cost (see Luke 9:57–62)

3. **Celebration**
    'Levi held a great banquet for Jesus at his house' (v. 29)

    •   for you
    •   for your friends

4. **Criticism**

    'The Pharisees and the teachers of the law complained' (v.30)

    •   Jesus criticised for the kind of people he mixed with
    •   Are we?

5. **Challenge**
    'It is not the healthy who need a doctor, but the sick' (v. 31)

    •   those who think they are healthy
    •   those who know they are sick

What kind of people does Jesus call? – **sinners to repentance** (v.32)

7. Living water
(John 4:1–42)

A SAMARITAN WOMAN – yet Jesus speaks to her and she learns:

1. **What Jesus offers**

   complete satisfaction (vv. 13–14)

   - internal

   - eternal

2. **What Jesus demands**

   - true repentance (vv. 16–18)

   - true worship (vv. 21–24)

3. **Who Jesus is**

   - a Jew (v. 9)

   - a prophet (v. 19)

   - the Messiah (vv. 25–26)

   - the Saviour of the world (v. 42)

8. Set free
(Mark 5:1–20)

'*LEGION*' – a demon–possessed man encounters the Son of God

1. **Ruin**
   The **work of Satan**

   - his **sphere of activity** : 1 John 5:19
   - his **purpose**   : John 10:10
   - his **strategy**   : 2 Corinthians 4:4

2. **Recognition**

   - **who** Jesus **is**
   - **why** Jesus **came** (1 John 3:8; Hebrews 2:14–15)

3. **Release**

Not only the **power** of Jesus, but also his **compassion.**

   - the **demons** are **expelled**
   - the **pigs** are **drowned**
   - the **man** is **set free** (John 8:36)

4. **Response**

   - **the people** beg Jesus to leave them – and he agrees
   - **the man** begs to go with Jesus – and he refuses

Now: victory at the cross (Colossians 2:13–15)
Not yet: final victory and judgement (1 Corinthians 15:20–28)

'*All down the ages, the world has been refusing Jesus because it prefers the pigs!*' (compare Luke 15:11–24)

9. Seeing and understanding
(Mark 8:22–26)

The context and nature of the miracle – seeing/understanding **who Jesus really is.**

1.   **Totally Blind**

   •   A distinguishing mark of **all** human beings (e.g. Saul of Tarsus (Acts 9)

   •   Only a **miracle from Jesus** will give sight.

2.   **Partial Sight**

   •   *'I see people... like trees walking'*

   •   The disciples only **partially understand** who Jesus is – vv. 29–32.

3.   **Full Vision**

   •   the **death and resurrection of Jesus** (v. 31) – the key to understanding clearly who Jesus is.

   •   the disciples only fully see **after Jesus is raised** – Luke 24:26.

The cost of **following** – vv. 34–35
The cost of **not** following – vv. 36–38
Do **you** see clearly who Jesus is?

10. The man who had everything yet lacked something
(Mark 10:17–34)

A man who **had everything**:
* young (Matthew 19:22)
* influential (Luke 18:18)
* wealthy (v. 22)
* moral (v. 20)

yet he **lacked something,** so he **came to Jesus**

1. **Sincerity (vv. 17–21)**
    *'a man **ran up** to him and **fell on his knees** before him'*

    Jesus **answers his question** with
    — a **question** – *'Who do you believe I am?'* (see 8:27)
    — a **reminder** – *'keep God's commandments'* (Exodus 20)

The young man **seems** to have kept God's laws (v. 20) but the **challenge of Jesus** (v. 21) leads to

2. **Sadness (vv. 22–23)**
    *'the man's **face fell**....he went away **sad**'*

    Jesus saw (v. 21) that he **lacked** (Matthew 19:20)
    — what he **had** – great wealth, which
    — he **loved more** than God (Exodus 20:3–5)
    The **love** of Jesus (v. 21) and his **sadness** (v. 23)

3. **Surprise (vv. 24–34)**
    *'the disciples were **amazed**....even **more amazed**....**astonished**'*

    — that **riches are a barrier** to heaven (v. 24–25)
    — that **no one can make** it into heaven (vv.26–27)
    — that Jesus **sets out for Jerusalem** (vv. 32–34)
    The **cost** – and the **reward** (vv. 28–31)

11. Achieving the impossible
(Luke 19:1–10)

ZACCHAEUS THE TAX–COLLECTOR (vv. 1–2) – a most unlikely candidate for salvation – until he encounters Jesus

The **process** :

1. **Curiosity** (vv. 3–4)

    • he wanted to see
    • he climbed a tree

2. **Call** (v. 5)

    • personal   (*'Zacchaeus'*)
    • urgent   (*'come down* **immediately***'*)
    • intimate   (*'I must* **stay at your house** *today'*)

3. **Change** (vv. 8–9)

    Zacchaeus responds immediately with joy

    • his **heart** is changed   (*'here and now I give...'*)
    • his **status** is changed   (*'a son of Abraham'*)

The mission of Jesus – still *'to seek and save the lost'* (v. 10)
See Revelation 3:20.

12. If only
(Luke 19:28–44)

The Passover Crowd – a tragic missed opportunity (v. 42)

The importance of **seeing with both eyes** who Jesus is

1. **Meekness and Majesty**
   The **identity** of Jesus:
   - the **king** – but not of this world (John 18:36)
   - the **servant** – to the cross   (Philippians 2:6–8)

   The **result** – *'Away with this man! Release Barabbas to us!'*

2. **Rejoicing and Weeping**
   A day of **mixed emotions**:
   - **joy**: in praise of Jesus
   - **sorrow**: for what lies ahead for Jerusalem

   Now the path ahead **divides sharply** –

3. **War and Peace**
   Judgement is certain
   - peace–terms refused (v. 42)
   - the Roman armies (vv. 43–44)

Final Warning!

- *'If only'* –   submit to the King while you can, or

- *'But now'* – face the consequences on his return.

13. From despair to hope
(John 20:1–18)

Mary Magdalene – an eye–witness of the resurrection.

1.   Devotion

- a debt of **love**   (Mark 16:9; Luke 8:2)
- a woman of **wealth**   (Luke 8:3)
- last at the **cross**   (Matthew 27:55–56)
- there at the **burial**   (Matthew 27:59–61)
- first at the **tomb**   (John 20:1)

2.   Confusion

- about the **death of Jesus**   (Mark 8:31–33)
- about the **resurrection of Jesus**   (vv. 13–15)

3.   Elation

- a personal **greeting** – *'Mariam'* (v. 16)
- a personal **response** – *'Rabboni'*

Two key themes (vv. 17–18)

The importance of the **ascension**
- *'my brothers'*
- *'my Father and your Father..my God and your God'*
  See Hebrews 7:25, 2:9–11

The importance of **evangelism** :
- *'go..and tell'*
- *'I have seen the Lord'*

14. Faith and sight
(John 20:19–31)

Thomas – the *'odd–one out'* when Jesus appears   (John 20:19–23).

The **relationship between faith and sight:**

1. **Seeing and Believing**
   'Unless I see...and put...I will not believe...'

   - **Jesus' answer** – *'Put your finger..reach out your hand..'*
   - **Thomas' response** – *'My Lord and my God.'*

2. **Not Seeing – Yet Believing**
   'Blessed are those who have not seen and yet have believed.'

   We have **all the evidence we need** (John 20:30–31)

   - accurate, eye-witness accounts (*'these things are written that you nay believe'*)
   - personal experience (*'by believing you may have life in his name.'*)

3. **Seeing – And yet not believing**
   'If they do not listen to Moses and the Prophets, they will not be convinced even if someone rises from the dead' (Luke 16:31)

   - someone **has risen** from the dead (1 Corinthians 15:1–11)
   - we have **the Scriptures** (Romans 10:9)
   - have we **repented**? (Acts 5:29–31)

Do we **believe**? Do we have **life**?

15. Reappointment in Galilee
(John 21)

Mark 16:6–7: a meeting arranged – for the disciples **and PETER.**

A day of memories by the Sea of Galilee

1. **Memories of miracles**

   • Luke 5:1–11 : a miraculous catch of fish

   • John 6:1–15 : bread and fish multiplied

2. **Memories of failure**

   • John 18:15–18, 25–27 : a charcoal fire

   • Mark 14:66–72 : a threefold denial

   The most important question : *'Do you truly love me?'*

Reappointment in Galilee : *'Follow me'* (Mark 1:16–17)

• from **fisherman** to **shepherd**

• a **personal** call :*'you must follow me.'*

16. A life-changing experience
(Acts 26)

Saul of Tarsus – a life–changing encounter on the road to Damascus

Four changes (from Acts 26:17–18)

1. From Darkness to Light

- the blind see (compare Luke 18:35–43)

2. From the Power of Satan to God

- the captives set free   (see John 8:31–47)

3. From Guilt to Forgiveness

- the guilty declared righteous (2 Corinthians 5:21)

4. From Persecution to Proclamation

- the new disciple commissioned (1 Timothy 1:12–14)

The example of Paul – **hope for anyone** (1 Timothy 1:15–16)

4

Treasure in Jars of Clay
(Studies in 2 Corinthians)

In 1968, Leslie Lyall, missionary statesman with the Overseas Missionary Society came to speak to a group of candidates preparing for overseas service. He stated that one book of the Bible would be especially valuable to us in the future. That book was, he claimed, Paul's second epistle to the church in Corinth.

I was very surprised for, although I had a good knowledge of the Bible, I had never found 2 Corinthians to be particularly helpful. However, I hadn't been in India for long before I began to appreciate his comment – and 2 Corinthians. And after twenty years in missionary service and seventeen in pastoral ministry I am more than ever convinced that 2 Corinthians is the book which resonates with all those involved in Christian service. In it we discover Paul the man as he reveals his heart and the hurts he encountered and the grace he discovered – made perfect in the weakness of all those who have been entrusted with the gospel – 'treasure in jars of clay'.

2 Corinthians is not an easy book to preach from for it is not as structured as say Romans or Ephesians. There is even a huge digression from 2:14 in which Paul does not resume his theme until 7:5! Some scholars have therefore questioned both the unity of the epistle and its authorship – see the books below for clear and convincing evidence against both arguments. 2 Corinthians is a book with many contrasts and, with this in mind, we have chosen titles for the sermons in the form of pairs of words.

Perhaps because of the reasons given, 2 Corinthians has been neglected by writers and commentators when compared with Paul's other epistles. Carson recommends C. K. Barrett (BNTC/HNTC, 1973) as 'quite outstanding'. Another major commentary is in the Word Biblical Commentary Series by Ralph P. Martin (Word, 1986). There is also *2 Corinthians* by Geoffrey Grogan in the *Focus*

on the Bible Commentary Series (Christian Focus). A useful paperback on the themes of 2 Corinthians is David Prior's *The Suffering and the Glory* (Hodder and Stoughton, 1985). Derek Prime's *Let's Study 2 Corinthians* (The Banner of Truth, 2000) is a valuable aid with useful questions for group study. On the issues raised in 2 Corinthians 10–13, Carson has written helpfully in *From Triumphalism to Maturity* (IVP, Baker, 1984).

1. Comfort and joy
(2 Corinthians 1:1–7)

The **background** to the letter – the model of a leader
Paul's **strategy** – to *'boast of his weakness'* (see 12:9–10)
The **key term** in the opening section – *'comfort'*

1. **Needing God's Comfort**

    The Christian is
    - **not exempt** from life's problems
    - **especially liable** to experience *'Christ's sufferings'*

See John 15:18–20; Acts 5:41; 2 Timothy 3:12; 1 Peter 4:12–13.

2. **Experiencing God's Comfort**

    The Christian **receives help** from
    - *'the Father of compassion'*
    - *'the God of all comfort'*
    - *'the God and Father of our Lord Jesus Christ'*
    The response – **praise!**

3. **Sharing God's Comfort**

    The Christian's sufferings are **productive**
    - **personally**
    - for **other sufferers**

within the *'fellowship'* of believers – absolute **security** (v. 7)

2. Despair and deliverance
(2 Corinthians 1:8–11)

Paul writes from **personal experience**

1. **Experience Shared (v. 8a)**
    'We do not want you to be uninformed, brothers,...'

    - sharing problems
    - with fellow–Christians

2. **Experience Described (vv. 8b–9a)**
    'Hardships..in the province of Asia' (Acts 19?)

    - overburdened to the point of breaking
    - no escape–route
    - the death–sentence?

3. **Experience Understood (v. 9b)**
    'But this happened....'

    - **self**–reliance – **'death'**
    - **divine** reliance – **life**

4. **Experience Anticipated (v. 10)**
    'on him we have set our hope....'

    - future **'deadly perils'**
    - future **divine deliverance** (see 4:7–12)

5. **Experience Shared (v. 11)**
    'as you help us...'

    - partnership in **prayer**
    - partnership in **praise**

3. Attack and defence
(2 Corinthians 1:12 – 2:11)

Another kind of suffering – **criticism from fellow Christians**.

Three tests for evaluating criticism:

1. **The test of CONSCIENCE in regard to our CONDUCT (1:12–14)**
    A clear conscience **verified by** –
    - **behaviour** – nothing to hide
    - **God's estimation** – not *'worldly wisdom'*

Paul's **hope** – that the Corinthians will **finally understand this**.

2. **The test of CONSISTENCY in regard to our MESSAGE (1:15–22)**
    The message Paul preached – **God keeps his word**
    - his **promises** – through his **Son**
    - his **presence** – through his **Spirit**

The preacher and his message – **no credibility–gap**.

3. **The test of CONCERN in regard to our CRITICS (1:23 – 2:11)**
    Paul did change his mind – but **for good motives** which showed
    - a **deep love** for them – to spare them (and him) more pain
    - a **willingness to forgive** – so Satan might not outwit them

His **Christlike concern** – not revenge but **reconciliation**.

4. Excommunication and restoration
(2 Corinthians 2:5–11)

The background – a case of **church discipline** (1 Corinthians 5?)

Two guiding principles for an authentic local church:**it should be:**

1.   **A Church which takes sin seriously**

The church is **a community of sinners** who are
*   **forgiven** by God (1 Corinthians 6:9–11)
*   **sensitive** to sin (1 John 1:8–9)
*   **concerned enough** for each other to exercise

discipline when all else has failed (Matthew 18:15–17)

The **primary goal** of discipline – **restoration**

2.   **A Church which offers forgiveness freely**

The **repentant offender** must be **fully restored** because
*   he might **otherwise 'drown'** in his sorrows
*   **this is right** *'in the sight of Christ'*
*   he **belongs to God's people** – not Satan

WARNING! **Watch out** for *'Satan's schemes'* to persuade us
*   to **treat sin lightly,** or
*   to **fail to experience (and offer) God's forgiveness**
The antidote – the **cross of Jesus**

5. Marketing and ministering
(2 Corinthians 2:12 – 3:6)

Paul uses **three vivid illustrations** to show the marks of **authentic Christian service:**

1. **The Triumphal Procession (2:12–14a)**

    •   Paul's **genuine concern** (vv. 12–13)

    •   Paul's **glad captivity** (v. 14a)

2. **The Fragrant Aroma (2:14b–17)**

    •   a **dividing ministry** (vv. 14b–16)

    •   an **undiluted message** (v. 17)

3. **The Letter of Recommendation (3:1–6)**

    •   divine **effectiveness** (vv. 1–3)

    •   divine **enabling** (vv. 4–6)

Conclusion – we should examine our

    •   **motives**

    •   **methods**

    •   **message**

in following and serving the Lord Jesus Christ

6. Old and new covenants
(2 Corinthians 3:7–18)

A battle for the hearts and minds of the Corinthian Christians
The **background**: Exodus 34:29–34 (the giving of the **old** covenant)

Three *'better effects'* of the **new** covenant

1.   **A change of VERDICT**

  •   the old covenant > **condemnation, death**

  •   the new covenant > **righteousness, life**

See Romans 8:1–4

2.   **A change of RELATIONSHIP**

  •   the old covenant >   **hidden, fear**

  •   the new covenant > **boldness, freedom**

See Hebrews 4:14–16, 10:19–22

3.   **A change of CHARACTER**

  •   the old covenant >   **external, fading**

  •   the new covenant > **inward, ever–increasing**

See Romans 12:1–2

God's **ultimate plan** for us – **GLORIFICATION** (Rom. 8:28–30)

7. Light and darkness
(2 Corinthians 4:1–6)

The **background** to Paul's understanding – his **own personal experience** (see Acts 26:9–18)

1.   **In the Dark**

   The problem of those who do not believe

   •   the veil (v. 3; see 3:14–15)

   •   blindness (v. 4; see John 9:35–41)

   Are you **still in the dark?**

2.   **Light in our Darkeness**

   Only God can make light shine in the darkness (v. 6)

   •   in creation (Genesis 1:3)

   •   in new creation (see 5:16–17)

   Have you *'seen the light'*?

3.   **Carrying the Light**

   God uses **human messengers** to carry the light (v. 1)

   •   to *'set forth the truth plainly'* –
      we must not change our **methods** (v. 2)

   •   to **preach 'Jesus Christ as Lord'** –
      we must not change the **message** (v. 5)

   Do others **see the** *'treasure in jars of clay'* (v. 7)?

8. Death and life
(2 Corinthians 4:7–18)

'We do not lose heart' (vv. 1 & 16) – even when the going gets tough, because of **two principles**:

1. **Death Before Life (vv. 7–12)**

   The **process of *'dying'***, like that of Jesus, is **beneficial**

   • for **us** – we experience the life of Christ

   • for **others** – they see the power of God

   • for **the glory of God** – he receives praise **on earth**

   A **present perspective** which keeps us going

2. **LIFE AFTER DEATH (vv. 13–18)**

   The **event of death**, like that of Jesus, is **beneficial**

   • for **us** – we will be raised from the dead

   • for **others** – they will join with us

   • for **the glory of God** – he receives praise **in heaven**

   A **future hope** which keeps us going

9. Buildings and tents
(2 Corinthians 5:1–5)

The picture used – an **exchange of residence**:

1. **Living in a Tent**

    The **human body is like a tent**:

    - **temporary accommodation** on earth
    - **damaged** by suffering and trouble
    - finally **destroyed**

    This is **true for all human beings** – including **Jesus** (see John 1:14; Hebrews 2:14–15)

2. **Longing for a Building**
    A new **resurrection body**:

    - designed and made **by God**
    - a **permanent structure** which will never wear out
    - designed **for heaven**

    A body **like that of the risen Jesus** (Philippians 3:20–21; see Luke 24:37–43)

3. **Leaving a Deposit**

    The **Holy Spirit** – the *'guarantee'*
    - the body – **a temple** (not a prison)
    - **'groaning'** in hope
    - **God's ultimate purpose** through *'all things'* (see Romans 8:18–30)

10. Home and away
(2 Corinthians 5:6–10)

The theme – **living in the present in the light of the future**

1. *'At home in the body; away from the Lord'* **(v. 6)**

   How we should **live now:**

   - with **confidence** (vv. 6–8)

   - by **faith** (v. 7)

   - to **please God** (v. 9)

2. *'Away from the body; at home with the Lord'* **(v. 8)**

   - we will **appear** before Christ's judgement–seat

   - we will **receive**

     — a **reward**, or

     — a **rebuke**

The final test – 1 Corinthians 3:10–15

11. Fear and love
(2 Corinthians 5:11–15)

Two motivating factors for the Christian:

1. The Fear of the Lord which cautions us (vv. 11–13)

A **future event** which influences the present

- everything apparent to God **on judgement–day** (v. 10)
- everything apparent to God **now** (v. 11)

So, we *'try to* **persuade** *people'*
- the importance of **the 'heart'** (not *'what is seen'*)
- the importance of **the mind** (see Acts 18:1–4)

2. The Love of Christ which compels us (vv. 14–15)

A **past event** which influences the present
- Christ **died for all**
- those who live, **live for him**

Driven by the love of Christ   (see Romans 5:5)

CONCLUSION :

- Christ is coming!
- keep on *'preaching'!* (see 2 Timothy 4:1–5)

12. Old and new
(2 Corinthians 5:16 – 6:2)

The coming of Jesus – the inauguration of a **new age**

1. **A New Situation – Reconciliation**

   The problem of separation from God resolved:
   - **divine initiative** from first to last (5:18)
   - **reconciling** the world (5:19)
   - through the **death of Jesus** (5:21)

   The solution brought about by *'God's grace'* (6:1)

2. **A New Creation – Regeneration**

   The **personal effects** of reconciliation (v. 17)
   - a change of **status**
   - a change of **nature**

   for *'anyone in Christ'*

3. **A New Obligation – Communication**

   A vital message to be communicated:
   - **Christ's ambassadors** – proclamation (5:20)
   - **God's fellow–workers** – persuasion (6:1)

   *'**Now** is the day of salvation'* (6:2; Isaiah 49:8)

   Don't miss out! (6:1)

13. Nothing and everything
(2 Corinthians 6:3–13)

No credibility–gap between the messenger and his message.
Three genuine marks of a servant of God:

1. **Steadfast in Suffering** (vv. 4b–5)
   'Great endurance'
   - in all kinds of **problems**
   - in all kinds of **opposition**
   - in all kinds of **deprivation**

Others see **God at work in us** through our response to suffering

2. **Christlike in Conduct** (vv. 6–7a)
   From **circumstances to conduct**
   - in **relation to others**
   - **integrity,** not pretence
   - **supernatural** in origin

Characteristic of **Jesus**

3. **Consistent in Conflict** (v. 7b–10)
   'The weapons of righteousness' (see Ephesians 6:10–20)
   - left hand – *'the shield of faith'* – **defence**
   - right hand – *'the sword of the Spirit'* – **attack**

The **only sure ground** – Christ's righteousness (see 5:21)

What is my life?

- am I a **stumbling–block to others** or do I **make them rich?**

- do I **commend** or **discredit** the message of Christ?

14. Temples and idols
(2 Corinthians 6:14 – 7:1)

The **implications** of being *'the temple of the living God'*

1. Prohibition (6:14 – 16a)

'Do not be yoked together with unbelievers' (Deuteronomy 22:10)
- different in **status**
- different in **understanding**
- different in **allegiance**
- different in **commitment**
- different in **worship**

Am I willing to say, 'No'?

2. Promises (6:16b – 18)

God's promises are **all fulfilled in Jesus** (see 1:20; 2 Peter 1:4)
- we are **the people of God** (Lev. 26:12; Isaiah 52:11; Jeremiah 32:38; Ezekiel 20:41; 37:27)

   'I will live with them'
   'I will walk among them'
   'I will receive you'
- we are **the family of God** (2 Samuel 7:14)

   'I will be a father to you'
   'you will be my sons and daughters'

Conclusion (7:1)
   'Since we have these promises..'
- *'let us purify ourselves'* – **decisive action** (negative)
- *'perfecting holiness'* – **continuous effort** (positive)

The result – intimacy with the Lord Almighty (see Matthew 5:8)

15. Remorse and repentance
(2 Corinthians 7:2–16)

Two contrasting kinds of sorrow (v. 10) when we are faced with our sin:
- *'worldly sorrow'* > **remorse**
- *'godly sorrow'* > **repentance**

1. **A different REACTION**
   - **remorse** focuses on **my suffering**
     - the law of cause and effect
     - unpleasant results
   - **repentance** focuses on **my sin**
     - painful effects also experienced but
     - my primary concern – God (e.g. Luke 15:17–19)

2. **A different RESPONSE**
   - **remorse** shows itself in **emotion**
     - tears?
   - **repentance** shows itself in **action** (see v. 11)
     - the *'fruits of repentance'* (see Luke 3:7–14; 19:8–9)

3. **A different RESULT**
   - **remorse** leads to **death**
     - breakdown of relationships
     - bitterness (see Hebrews 12:15–17)
     - despair (e.g. Judas Iscariot – Matthew 27:3–5)
   - **repentance** leads to **salvation**
     - reconciliation (v. 7)
     - no regrets
     - hope (e.g. Peter – John 21:15–19)

16. Rich and poor
(2 Corinthians 8:1–15)

Background: Paul's appeal to the Corinthians to give more to his relief– fund for poor believers in Judaea (see Acts 11:27–30; Galatians 2:8–10; 1 Corinthians 16:1–14; Romans 15:26–27)

Thoughts on giving (one of the marks of genuine repentance)

1. **Think of other generous givers   (vv. 1–5)**

    The **giving of the Macedonian Christians** was

    - sacrificial   (vv. 1–3)
    - enthusiastic   (v. 4)
    - spiritually motivated (v. 5)

2. **Think of your own half–hearted giving (vv. 6–8, 10–12)**

    The **giving of the Corinthian Christians** was

    - lacking (vv. 6–8)
    - incomplete (vv. 10–12)

3. **Think of other needy believers (vv. 13–15)**

    - the **needs** of the **Christians in Judaea could be met by**
    - the **plenty** of the **Christians in Corinth**

4. **Think of the greatest giver of all   (v. 9)**

    The **grace of the Lord Jesus Christ**

    - took **him** from **riches to poverty**
    - took **us** from **poverty to riches**

17. Ready and willing
(2 Corinthians 8:16 – 9:5)

Understanding the principles behind Paul's relief fund for the Christians in Judaea:

1. **How was the appeal viewed?**
   Not a peripheral issue but **central to the gospel** of Christ (8:9)

   - as *'honouring to the Lord'* (8:19)

   - as a *'service to the saints'* (9:1, 8:4)

   A **proof of love** – for the Lord and fellow–Christians (8:24)

2. **HOW WAS THE COLLECTION ADMINISTERED?**
   The choice of **three men** (8:16–18, 22)

   - of proven reputation

   - of earnest commitment

   The need for **scrupulous care** (8:20–21)

3. **HOW WAS THE MONEY RAISED?**
   Paul **encourages the Corinthians** (9:5)

   - to give generously, not sparingly

   - to give gladly, not grudgingly

   Such giving is **infectious**

18. Sowing and reaping
(2 Corinthians 9:6–15)

The **principle** (v. 6) – sowing and reaping
The **results of generous sowing**:

1. **Deepened fellowship between Christians**

    An opportunity to **demonstrate Christian love** between
    - **very poor** Christians from a **Jewish background** in Jerusalem and Judaea, and
    - **more affluent** Christians from a **Gentile background** in Corinth and Greece

2. **Increased thanksgiving to God**

    God is praised (v. 11) by
    - those who **receive the gift** (v. 12)
    - those who **witness doctrine in action** (v. 13)

3. **OVERFLOWING ABUNDANCE TO THE GIVER**

Generous sowing leads to **generous reaping** (see Luke 6:38)
- God provides **all you need** (vv. 8–10) – and more
- so that you can **give more** (v. 11a)

The circle is **completed by giving** but **broken by selfishness**

PRACTICAL GUIDELINES (v. 7)
- give **personally**
- give **thoughtfully**
- give **cheerfully**

Above all, **give generously** – we have a **very generous God** (v. 15) – let us **be like Him!**

19. Timid and bold
(2 Corinthians 10:1–11)

(2 Corinthians 10–13 reflects a deterioration in the situation at Corith. Bad news has reached the Apostle Paul, causing him to write in a more sombre tone).

He **depicts the Christian life as warfare in which we must...**

1. **Identify the opposition (vv. 2, 7, 11)**
   compare 11:13–15

2. **Enter the battlefield** (vv. 4–5)
   compare Romans 12:1–2

3. **Select our weapons** (vv. 4–5)
   compare Ephesians 6:10–18; Romans 1:16

4. **Determine our strategy**

   • a **gentle appeal** (vv. 1–2, 7–10; cf Matthew 11:28–30)

   • **decisive action** (vv. 2, 6, 11; compare Mark 11:15–17)

20. Classification and commendation
(2 Corinthians 10:12–18)

Paul's defence (*'boast'*) against his critics.
He will not *'play by their rules'* (v. 12) but by **God's criteria**:

1. Personal responsibility   (vv. 13–15a)

Paul's *'field'* – given by God (Acts 26:17–18)
- his **agreed area of ministry** – to the Gentile world, including Corinth (see Galatians 2:6–9)
- for which he is **accountable** (3:1–3)

Contrast the *'super–apostles'* – **intruders** and **unaccountable**

2. Global opportunity   (v. 15b–16)

Paul's vision – to plant the gospel in virgin territory
- in **Corinth** (Acts 18)
- from Corinth to *'regions beyond'* (see Rom. 15:17–24)

Contrast the *'super–apostles'* – **building on another's foundation**

3. Final accountability (vv. 17–18)

The **Lord's approval**
- at the **last judgement** (5:9–11)
- in **present ministry**

Paul's **ultimate *'boast'*** (Jeremiah 9:23–24) – see **Galatians 6:14**

21. True and false
(2 Corinthians 11:1–15)

The **dangers of deception:**

1. **Do not be deceived by SUPERFICIAL APPEARANCES**

   Satan and his agents are **masters of disguise** (vv. 13–15)
   - focus on the **medium** (*'trained speaker'*), rather than
   - the **message** (*'knowledge'*) – see v. 5

   The Lord looks at *'the heart'* (1 Samuel 16:7)

2. **Do not be deceived by SPECIOUS ARGUMENTS**

   The **battle for the mind** (see 10:3–5)
   - the **first deception** (Genesis 3)
   - the **same strategy** repeated – see vv. 3–4

   'Jesus plus' always equals *'Jesus minus'*

3. **Do not be deceived by SUPERIOR ATTITUDES**

   The *'super apostles'* **lord it over** the Corinthians (Mark 10:
   42–45), but Paul's attitude **reflects that of the Lord**
   - the **humble servant** who is **modelled on his master**
     (vv. 7–10)
   - the **loving father** who is **jealous for his daughter**
     (verse 2)

   No wonder his words (vv. 13–15) are **so strong!**

22. Foolish and wise
(2 Corinthians 11:16–33)

Paul *'boasts'* – he compares himself to his rivals in three ways

1. **Leadership Style   (vv. 19–21a)**

   - they were authoritarian
   - Paul says he is *'too weak for that'*

2. **Ethnic Origins   (vv. 21b–22)**

   - they were Hebrews – descendants of Abraham
   - Paul says *'So am I!'* (but see Philippians 3:4b–9)

3. **Personal Achievements (vv. 23–33)**

   - they claimed to be successful servants of Christ
   - Paul lists *'things that show my weakness'*

TO THINK ABOUT

- What kind of leader am I?
- Where do I place my security?
- How honest am I in my Christian discipleship?

23. Weak and strong
(2 Corinthians 12:1–10)

A lesson **learned through adversity** – *'when I am weak, I am strong'*

1. **An Ecstatic Experience** (vv. 1–6)
   The realm of *'visions and revelations'*
   - **personal** – about Paul himself (*'a man in Christ'*)
   - **particular** – fourteen years ago
   - *'paradise'* – in God's presence in heaven
   Yet Paul gives **no details** of what he saw and heard

2. **A Painful Problem** (v. 7)
   A *'thorn in my flesh'*
   - its **nature**
     spiritual?
     physical?
     human?
   - its **origin**
     a *'messenger from Satan'*
     'given me' (from God)

3. **A Powerful Principle** (vv. 8–10)
   A **prayer request refused** so that Paul would
   - experience **God's grace** in his need
   - display **God's power** in his weakness
   Not just acceptance but also **delight**

'He has said' (v. 9)
   - the way of Christ (Matthew 26:36–46)
   - the way of the cross (13:4)

24. Parents and children
(2 Corinthians 12:11–21)

Paul has addressed the **false teachers**; now he addresses the **Corinthians**

They were **failing in four areas**

1. **Failing to recognise true apostolic authority (vv. 11–12)**

   • Paul had demonstrated signs and wonders
   • But he had also shown great endurance

2. **Failing to trust Paul's financial integrity (vv. 13–18)**

   • they said he was unprofessional
   • they suggested he might be a con–man!

3. **Failing to grow out of spiritual immaturity (vv. 19–20)**

   • they had been well taught (see 1 Corinthians 12–13)
   • but there were still divisions

4. **Failing to deal with serious immorality (v. 21)**

   • there was a lax attitude to doctrine
   • which resulted in casual attitudes in moral issues

Conclusion

   • Paul was humbled
   • But would the Corinthians repent?

25. Building up and tearing down
(2 Corinthians 13:1–10)

Jesus is **Lord** (Philippians 2:9–11)
Paul has **delegated authority** in Corinth (v. 10)

The character of a **godly leader** seen in these verses:

1. **Paul's promise (vv. 1–4)**

   A **final warning!**
   - second visit – **'weak'**
   - third visit – **'strong'**
   The way of **Christ** – the way of **the servant**

2. **Paul's preference (vv. 5–9a)**

   'Examine yourselves' – *'do it yourself discipline'*
   - if **the Corinthians** pass the test then
   - **Paul** will pass the test and so
   - they will **accept his authority and discipline**
   Paul's **primary concern** – their welfare (and not his reputation)

3. **Paul's prayer (vv. 9b–10)**

   His prayer reveals his **true attitude** to the Corinthians
   - not **punishment** (*'tearing down'*) but
   - **'perfection'** (*'building up'*)
   The **'building–work'** goes on (Matt 16:18; Ephesians 2:19–22)

26. Love and peace
(2 Corinthians 13:11–14)

Paul's **final concern** – for **harmony** (*'love and peace'*) in the church at Corinth (John 13:34–35):

1.   The goal of love and peace
    Human obedience required

> **wholehearted commitments** to love and peace (v. 11a)
> * *'aim for perfection'*
>
> * *'listen to my appeal'*
>
> * *'be of one mind'*
>
> * *'live in peace'*

> **outward expressions** of love and peace (vv. 12–13)
> * *'the holy kiss'*
>
> * *'greetings from all the saints'*

2.   The God of love and peace
    Divine help assured

> * a **promise** (v. 11b)
>
> * a **prayer** (v. 14)
>   * *'the grace of the Lord Jesus Christ'*
>
>   * *'the love of God'*
>
>   * *'the fellowship of the Holy Spirit'*

> *'be with you* **all***'*

5

Running away from the Lord
(Studies in the Book of Jonah)

The Old Testament Book of Jonah merits careful study and application on several levels.

The first is on an historical level – despite doubts of many critics who would reduce it to an allegory or parable on the supposed impossibility of a man being swallowed by a fish and living to tell the tale! However, the only Old Testament reference to Jonah outside of the book which bears his name (in 2 Kings 14:25) places him at a crucial time in Israel's history, with the nation's security threatened by the rising superpower, Assyria. Hence Jonah's reluctance to go and preach in Nineveh and offer possible salvation to Israel's enemy. Any of the standard commentaries – ranging from Calvin (1559, published Banner of Truth, 1986) and Hugh Martin (1870, published Banner of Truth 1958) up to present-day commentaries, such as the Tyndale Old Testament Commentary (T. Desmond Alexander, 1988) deal competently with the text and application on this level.

On another level, Jonah can be seen and preached as a picture of the Church – like Israel, running away from her God-given call to preach the gospel, asleep in the storms of life while the heathen are on their knees praying for rescue. R. T. Kendall's series of sermons is a challenging and helpful exposition of Jonah from this perspective (Hodder & Stoughton, 1978).

Thirdly, Jonah can be taken as a picture of an individual Christian who is, in the words of the title of the series 'running away from the Lord' – seeking to escape the divine calling on his or her life (though usually for different reasons from Jonah). A fascinating and well-written book which applies this theme to Christian ministers is Eugene Peterson's *Under the Unpredictable Plant*.

Finally, the story of Jonah inside the fish is quoted by the Lord Jesus Christ as a sign of the period he will be 'in the heart of the

earth' after his death and before his resurrection, and also of the repentance of the men of Nineveh who will be an indictment on judgement-day of the unbelief of the people of Israel to 'one greater than Jonah' (see Matthew 12:39–42, 16:4; Luke 11:29–32). Any good commentary on the gospels will draw out the meaning and implication of these verses.

1. The word of the Lord
(1:1–2)

The Book of Jonah – one of the Minor **Prophets**

- a message to the **nation of Israel**
- a message to the **Church**
- a message about **Jesus** (Matthew 12:38–41)

A story about **the LORD**

1. **He is the God who SPEAKS**
   God **has spoken**
      - in **creation** (Genesis 1:3)
      - through the **prophets**, like Jonah
      - finally, through **his Son** (John 1:1; Hebrews 1:1–2)
   He **still speaks** – through the Holy Spirit (see John 16:7–8)

2. **He is the God who SENDS**
   His **messengers** are
      - human, and so
      - flawed (see 1:3)
   Yet he **still he perseveres** with them (see 3:1)

3. **He is the God who SEES**
   The **affairs of the world** are seen by the Lord
      - cities and nations
      - individuals

His word **speaks against** wickedness – an **opportunity for repentance and salvation** (see 3:6–10)

2. Heading in the wrong direction
(1:3)

The **dynamics of disobedience**

1. **The rejection of Nineveh**

    Jonah **refuses to go** to Nineveh

    • his **problem** – theological, doubting God's goodness (see Genesis 3:1–5)

    • his **solution** – practical, running away in the opposite direction

    But he cannot **resign from the Lord's service**

2. **The attraction of Tarshish**

    Jonah **heads for Tarshish** which promises

    • untold **wealth** and **satisfaction** (see 2 Chronicles 9:21)

    • an **escape** from *'the face of the Lord'*

    But it is all **an illusion**

3. **The connection of Joppa**

    Jonah **arrives at Joppa** and finds

    • a **ship** going to Tarshish

    • a **berth** he can purchase

    It **seems providential**, but it is **wrong** (see 1 Samuel 24:4, 26:8)

    (Has Jonah escaped? – see 1:4–6 – *'When God sends a storm')*

3. When God sends a storm
(1:4–6)

No escape from the Lord, who *'hurls'* a great wind
- **directed** at Jonah
- the sailors **affected**

In order to bring **both to repentance and salvation**

Contrasting effects in the storm:

1. **The sailors afraid**
   Their lives are **threatened**
   - desperate **prayers**
   - desperate **measures**

   But all **to no avail**

2. **The prophet asleep**
   Jonah **'out of commission'**, so he is
   - a **curse** to the sailors, instead of
   - a **blessing** (contrast Acts 27:21–26; see 1 Peter 3:15–16)

   The storm revealed Jonah to be **a prophet who did not pray**

Conclusion
Another storm and **another sleeper** – Mark 4:35–41
One **'greater than Jonah'** who is
- **able** to help
- **willing** to help

when we **call out for help**

4. Found out by God
(1:7–12)

The process by which Jonah's rebellion is ended:

1. **Investigation (v. 7)**
    The **casting of lots** in order to
    •   **discover** the truth from God (Proverbs 16:33)
    •   **expose** Jonah's guilt (see John 16:7–8)
    Now, at last, Jonah **has to give** an

2. **Explanation (vv. 8–10)**
    Jonah **confesses**
    •   who he **is** – a Hebrew
    •   who he **worships** – the Lord
    The sailors are **terrified** and seek from Jonah a

3. **Resolution (vv. 11–12)**
    Jonah has **the answer** to the crisis
    •   **confession** of guilt before men
    •   **consecration** of himself before God
The **only means of salvation** – for Jonah and the sailors

The example of Jesus
    •   *'not guilty'*
    •   *'not my will'*
The principle of **spiritual worship and service** – see
Romans 12:1–2

5. Saved
(1:11–17)

The **salvation of the sailors** – a picture of **God's salvation in Christ**.

1. **The MEANS of salvation (v. 11)**
   The sailors **need a *'preacher'*** (Romans 10:12–15)
   - the Lord uses **Jonah**
   - despite his **disobedience**

   The mystery of God's **amazing providence** (Romans 11:33–36)

2. **The MESSAGE of salvation (v. 12)**
   Jonah **explains *'the way of salvation'***
   - the **cause** of the crisis – **sin**
   - the **solution** of the crisis – **sacrifice**

   The **message of the gospel** – John 3:16; Romans 6:23

3. **The MOMENT of salvation (vv. 13–15)**
   Two steps must be taken
   - the **abandonment** of **human effort**
   - the **acceptance** of **God's remedy**

   The result – peace (Romans 5:1)

CONCLUSION

- The **sailors** become **worshippers** (v. 16)
- **Jonah** is **also saved** (v. 17)

6. Inside the whale
(1:17– 2:2)

Jonah is *'being saved'*.
The Lord's plan – to **restore him to service.**
Three phases:

1. **Going Down**
    Disobedience – the **downward path:**
    *   down to **Joppa**
    *   down into **the ship**
    *   down into **the sea**
    At last Jonah **reaches**

2. **Rock Bottom**
    The Lord **provides** *'a great fish'* *for*
    *   Jonah's **salvation**
    *   Jonah's **restoration**
    Now Jonah is in the **right place**

3. **Looking Up**
    Finally, Jonah *'prays to the Lord his God'*
    *   he *'looks again'*
    *   to the Lord's *'holy temple'*
    The *'second look'* (2:4) precedes the *'second call'* (3:1–2)

'One Greater than Jonah'

*   a greater **sign** (Matthew 12:39–40)

*   a greater **salvation** (Hebrews 7:25)

Look to Christ! Look again!

7. A surprising prayer in a strange place
(2:1–9)

All we know of Jonah's experience inside the fish – *'he prayed'* (2:1)

1. A Strange Place
Unique circumstances:

- in the belly of the fish
- enclosed by the Lord
- at last he prays (contrast 1:6)

A *'near–death'* **experience** – compare 2 Corinthians 1:8–10

2. A Surprising Prayer

Surprising for **two reasons**:

- its **origin** – from the Psalms (Psalm 18, 120, 42, 31, 5, etc.)
  compare **Matthew 27:46** with Psalm 22:1 and Luke 23:46 with Psalm 31:5

- its **optimism** (thanksgiving, not lament)
  Jonah's priority is spiritual, not physical
A new and better hope – Hebrews 4:14–16

8. Salvation comes from the Lord
(2:8–10)

The **central theme** of the Book of Jonah – and of the Bible
'Good theology learned in a strange college'
Only **two possible opinions** about this statement:

1. **The Foolishness of Idolatry**
Foolish **because**
   * they are worthless (*'lying vanities'*)
   * they prevent access to the grace of God

   The **problem** – *'clinging'* to idols

2. **The Wisdom of Worship**
Jonah's response to the Lord's salvation
   * **a song** of thanksgiving
   * **a vow** of commitment

   Yet he is **still inside the fish**!

'THE SIGN OF JONAH' (see Matthew 12:38–41; Luke 11:29–32)
Salvation demonstrated – for Jonah and **through Jesus**
   * a greater **person**
   * a greater **miracle**
The **conclusion** – **no excuse for failing to repent**

9. A second chance

(3:1–3)

A **second call** – and a **second chance**

Lessons learned about the Lord (between Jonah 1:1 and Jonah 3:1):

1. **The Unchanging Purpose of the Lord**

    The **Lord's plans** have not changed:

    *   the same **message** – God's judgement
    *   the same **medium** – *'preach'* (1 Corinthians 1:21)
    *   the same **messenger** – Jonah

2. **The Unlimited Patience of the Lord**

    The **Lord's love** for Jonah shown:

    *   despite his disobedience
    *   in going to extreme lengths to bring him back

    Don't mistake his **patience** for **impotence** (2 Peter 3:9–12)

3. **The Unfathomable Providence of the Lord**

    The Lord **uses everything** to further his plans – **even Jonah's sin**:

    *   to make him **a *'sign'*** of God's grace (1 Timothy 1:12–17)
    *   to make him **willing to go** to Nineveh (v. 3a)

    Incomprehensible to human minds – Romans 11:33–36

10. Mission to Nineveh
(3:3–4)

NINEVEH – a city under judgement – yet they are totally unaware of it.
Their only hope – a message *'from outside'* – from the Lord.

1. **Commission**
   God uses **a human voice** –
   - **Jonah** – to Nineveh (1:1–2, 3:1–2)
   - **Jesus** – to the world (Hebrews 1:1–2)
   - **disciples** – to the nations (Matthew 28:18–20; 24:14)

   The importance of **obedience.**

2. **Communication**
   The **message** – the *one 'called out '* calls out
   - **divine authentication** – they *'believed God'* (v. 5, see 1 Thessalonians 1:4–5)
   - **judgement on all** – the whole city (see Luke 13:1–5)

   The importance of **proclamation.**

3. **Compassion**
   The Lord gives an **opportunity for repentance** (*'forty days'*)
   - he **cares for** the city (v. 3)
   - he **sends** the prophet
   - he *'sets a day'* (see Acts 17: 29–31)

   The importance of **response** (2 Corinthians 5:20 – 6:2)

11. Life-saving changes
(3:5–10)

Jonah's message – **bad news for Nineveh**
But **disaster is avoided** through **three life–saving changes**:

1. **A Change of Mind –** they *'believed God'*
    A surprising response from the people of Nineveh:
    *   they **heard and understood** the message of judgement
    *   they **believed and accepted** it to be true (from God)
    Repentance – a change of mind
    (see Matthew 3:2, 4:17; Acts 2:37–38)

2. **A Change of Direction –** they *'called urgently on God'*
    New priorities for the whole population
    *   **fasting** – from food & drink **and sin** (see Isaiah 58)
    *   **serious petition** to God (see Luke 18:10–14)
    An **uncertain outcome** – *'who knows...?'*

3. **A 'Change' of heart – God** *'had compassion and did not bring on them the destruction he had threatened'*
    God's response to what he saw
    *   mercy shown
    *   judgement averted

Through the death and resurrection of Jesus, we have
*   **a better way** of salvation (John 3:16–18)
*   **less excuse** at judgement (Matthew 12:38–41)

12. Something greater than Jonah
(Matthew 12:38–41)

Jesus **compares himself with Jonah:**

1. A Greater Message

Jonah	– judgement	(Jonah 3:4)
Jesus	– salvation	(John 3:16–17)

2. A Greater Messenger

Jonah	– human	(Jonah 1:1)
	– disobedient	(Jonah 1:3)
	– a prophet	(Jonah 3:4)
Jesus	– divine	(John 1:1–3)
	– obedient	(Philippians 2:5–8)
	– Saviour	(1 Peter 2:24)

3. A Greater Miracle

Jonah	– alive inside the fish	(Jonah 1:17)
	– brought out again	(Jonah 2:10)
Jesus	– dead and buried	(Luke 23:50–55)
	– raised from the dead	(Matt.28:1–10)

Conclusion
The Ninevites repented yet we have *'something greater'*
therefore

- **no excuse** for unbelief (Luke 16:27–31)

- *'God now commands* **all people everywhere to repent***'* (Acts 17:29–31)

- *'***now** *is the day of salvation'* (2 Corinthians 6:1–2)

13. Angry with God
(Jonah 4:1–5)

Jonah's anger – a **surprising reaction**

1. **Jonah anger explained (v. 1)**
   The reason – because Nineveh was not destroyed
   - Jonah discredited as a prophet?
   - no warning for Israel?
   - the Lord's inclusion of the Gentiles

   Jonah – confused and **angry with God**

2. **Jonah's anger expressed (vv. 2–3)**
   Jonah **pours out his complaint** to the Lord
   - a simmering resentment going back to his call (1:1–2)
   - confirmed by the Lord's compassion to Nineveh
   - now he wants to die (contrast his prayer in Chapter 2)

'It was not a theological error that ignited his anger but a **spiritual poverty**' (Eugene Peterson)

3. **Jonah's Anger Examined (vv. 4–5)**
   The **Lord's answer** to Jonah
   - a question to make Jonah think
   - about his own experience of the Lord

   Jonah still waits for **judgement** – but God shows **mercy** (see Ephesians 2:4–9)

14. A lesson from the Lord
(Jonah 4:5–11)

Jonah is **angry** – with the Lord
The Lord is **'slow to anger and abounding in love'** – to Jonah
Three stages in *'a lesson in love'*

1. **Comprehension – understanding**
   The Lord uses a striking **object–lesson:**
   - a vine
   - a worm
   - a scorching east wind

   Not just **theory** but also **experience**

2. **Compassion – feeling**
   Jonah is **upset and angry**
   - about the **vine**
   - but **not** about the **Ninevites** (and cattle?)

Passion wants sin **punished; compassion** wants sin **pardoned**

3. **Commission – acting**
   God's compassion **made known by human beings:**
   - **Jonah (**1:2; 2:2)
   - **Jesus** (1 John 4:9–10)
   - **disciples** (Matthew 28:18–20)

*'Should **I** not be concerned...'* – *'should **you** not be concerned..?'*

6

Crying in the wilderness
(Studies in the life of John the Baptist)

The figure of John the Baptist bridges the Old and New Testaments – an authentic prophetic voice speaking after a two hundred year period of silence to fulfil the final prophecy of the Old Testament coming in the spirit and power of Elijah (Malachi 4:5–6).

His brief career, summarily extinguished by the fickleness of Herod and the vindictiveness of a woman ('a lamp that burned') fulfilled its divine purpose to 'prepare the way for the Lord' (Isaiah 40:3).

He is a shining example of dedication to the task to which God called him, gladly willing to sublimate his own ambitions to one far greater – 'the thongs of whose sandals I am not worthy to untie'. Yet he is also revealed as one who is also human – how many of us have not identified with his experience 'in doubting-castle'?

Our Lord Jesus Christ commends him in the highest terms – 'among those born of women there has not risen anyone greater than John the Baptist' – yet then adds the surprising and challenging words 'yet he who is least in the kingdom of heaven is greater than he' (Matthew 11:11). Great privileges and great responsibility – which is why John the Baptist merits careful study – and imitation.

Different aspects of his career are described by all four Gospel writers and again there are many excellent commentaries – old and new – which will explain the text. I am not aware of any specific book devoted to him alone – which is probably appropriate given his words – 'he must increase, but I must decrease.' Tom Houston's book *Characters Around the Cradle* devotes ten chapters to a study of John the Baptist (CFP).

1. Promise fulfilled
(Luke 1:1–25)

God always **keeps his promises** (Numbers 23:19)

1. Silence

Between the Testaments – the *'silent years'* . **Times of silence**:

- in history
- in personal experience

What do the faithful do at these times? They **'wait'** (Psalm 27:13–14)

2. Speech

Through an angel, God gives a **message of good news** for
- Zechariah and Elizabeth : a son
- The people of Israel : *'Elijah'* to prepare the way for the Lord (see Malachi 3:1; 4:5–6)

3. Dumbness

Zechariah's **unbelief**. But are **you and I**

- **believing** God's better Word? (Hebrews 1:1–3; 3:12)
- **silent**? (the sign of unbelief)

Conclusion :God still achieves his purposes (see Esther 4:14)

A wonderful example of willingness : Luke 1:26–38

2. In God's prenatal class
(Luke 1:57–66)

The **gestation-period**: between conception and birth.

In *'God's prenatal class'* in a

- broad historical sense
- narrow personal sense

An opportunity for **learning**:

1. **Learning to wait for God's time**
   God's **perfect timing** (see Acts 1:7–8):
   - in our **lives**
   - in our **world**

2. **Learning to understand God's character**

   Personal experience of God through
   - blessing   (Elizabeth)
   - adversity   (Zechariah)

   The **most important lesson** –   *'The Lord is gracious'*

3. **Learning to proclaim God's deeds**
   Zechariah: from **dumbness to praise** (see vv. 67–79)
   The effect on his hearers:

   - awe   (Genesis 28:16–17;   Isaiah 6:5;   Luke 5:8–9)
   - anticipation   (Romans 8:28–39)

3. Prepare the way for the Lord
(Luke 3:1–18)

The work of **preparation** for God's greatest act in human history

1. **Identification**

   'I am the voice of one calling...' (see Isaiah 40:3–5)

   - John's **appearance** and **lifestyle** (Matthew 3:4)
   - John's **identity** (John 1:19–23)

2. **Proclamation**

   *'..**preaching** a baptism of repentance for the forgiveness of sins'*

   - **radical** change – every obstacle removed
   - **specific** change – for each individual

   The **proof** – *'fruit in keeping with repentance'*

3. **Anticipation**

   '..one more powerful than I **will come**'

   - the **herald** and the **Messiah**
   - **water** and **Spirit** (and **fire**)

The **fulfilment** – Acts 2. Have you **repented** and **believed**?

The **final fulfilment** – 2 Peter 3. Are you **ready**?

4. The friend of the bridegroom
(John 1:29–43; 3:22–36)

When Jesus is baptised, John **recognises him** as:

1. The Servant, who does the Father's will

- **more worthy** than John, yet
- **identifying** with sinners

2. The Messiah, who baptises with the Holy Spirit
Jesus the *'Anointed One'*

- the Spirit's **fullness**
- the Spirit's **permanence** (*'remain'*)
- the Spirit's **outpouring** (Acts 2)

3. The Son, whom the Father loves

- the **divine Son** (Matthew 16:16–17; 1 John 4:14–15)
- the **Father's love** (John 3:16)

4. The Lamb, who takes away the sin of the world

- the lamb of the Old Testament
- the sin of the world – for **those who believe**

'The Friend of the Bridegroom' (John 3:28–29)

- John points others to **the Bridegroom who is seeking a bride** (Ephesians 5:25–27)

- **The invitations** are going out for *'the wedding supper of the Lamb'* (Revelation 19:6–9). **Have you replied?**

5. In doubting castle
(Matthew 11)

Doubt – *'faith in two minds'*
Doubt caused by

1. The pressure of difficult circumstances

John's **situation**:
* *'in prison'*
* unable to continue his work

The **solution** :ask Jesus (v. 2)

2. The disappointment of unfulfilled expectations

* the **context**: the miracles of Jesus (see Luke 7:11–17)
* the **question**: *'Are you the one who was to come..?'* (v 3)
* the **answer**: God's Word fulfilled (Isaiah 35:5–6, 61:1)

3. The fear of a wasted life

* **different ministries** of Jesus and John (vv. 16–18)
* high commendation for **faithfulness** (vv. 7–11)

CONCLUSION

* a **warning** against unbelief (vv. 20–24, see v. 11)
* an **invitation** to all (vv. 28–30)

'Should we expect someone else?' – **there is no–one else**

6. A lamp that burned
(Mark 6:12–29)

Herod's birthday – *'the opportune time'* (v. 21)

Four main characters:

1. **John the Baptist: A fearless preacher**
   - the **message**: v. 18
   - the **cost**: v. 17

2. **Herodias: A vindictive woman**
   - nursing a **grudge**: v. 19, and
   - looking to **kill** (cf. Jezebel – 1 Kings 19:2)

3. **Herod : A weak man**
   - he feared **his wife**: vv. 17–18, and
   - he feared **John**: v. 20

4. **Salome : A willing accomplice**
   - exploiting the **opportunity**: v. 22
   - seizing their **chance**: vv. 24–28

The Big Question :why did God allow it?

   - we live in a fallen world: Hebrews 11:32–40

   - our times are in God's hands (Psalm 139:16) :
   - respond while you can (see Luke 23:1–12)
   - *'burn'* for the Lord (John 5:31–36)

   - there is a day of reckoning :Revelation 20:11–15

7

God meant it for good
(Studies in the life of Joseph)

The story of Joseph is one of the best-known in the Bible – not least because of the musical *'Joseph and His Amazing Technicolor Dreamcoat'* by Andrew Lloyd-Webber. While the music may be singable and the lyrics memorable, sadly the story departs markedly from that of the Biblical record in Genesis 37–50. This is not just in the detail of the Technicolour coat (the Hebrew word is obscure and probably means 'long-sleeved' rather than 'many-coloured' but more fundamentally in the philosophy which underlies it.

In the musical, when Joseph is finally elevated from prison to Prime Minister, the message is 'anyone from anywhere at any time can make it if they get a lucky break'. Nothing could be further from the truth which Joseph declared to his petrified and guilty brothers: 'You intended to harm me, but God intended it for good to accomplish what is now being done, the saving of many lives' (Genesis 50:20). Or, in the words of the Authorised Version of the Bible – 'God meant it for good.'

The providence of God which is seen in the life of Joseph is all the more remarkable in view of the fact that he is not reassured by direct encounters and words from the Lord as were his father, Jacob, his grandfather, Isaac, and his great-grandfather, Abraham. Perhaps he did not need them for his faith remains resolute through all the adverse personal circumstances he faces. There is much we can learn from him for the Christian has far greater reason to believe that 'in all

things God works for the good of those who love him' (Romans 8:28).

Some commentators (especially, though not exclusively, older ones) have idealised the character of Joseph, even going so far as to see him as a 'type of Christ'. Other more modern ones have gone to the opposite extreme – picturing him as a spoiled child who foolishly boasted in front of his older brothers and almost merited their ill-treatment.

Probably the truth is somewhere between so that we can both identify with Joseph's weaknesses and learn from his maturing, while at the same time being challenged by his faith and seeking to emulate it.

The Word Biblical Commentary on Genesis by Gordon Wenham (Word, 1994), the Bible Speaks Today on Genesis 12–50 by Joyce Baldwin (IVP, 1986) and *Creation and Change* by Douglas Kelly (Christian Focus) are helpful on the text. Derek Kidner (IVP, 1967) is a model of concise exegesis and memorable comments, while William Still's *Theological Studies in Genesis and Romans* (Christian Focus, 2000) has helpful comments on the text and application for the expositor.

Books devoted to Joseph range from the nineteenth century with George Lawson's *The Life of Joseph* 1807, republished Banner of Truth, 1972) to R. T. Kendall's *God Meant it for Good* (Tyndale, 1986). *Living with your Dreams* by David Seamands (Scripture Press, 1980) is a more novel approach which some will find more helpful than others. *A Refuge For My Heart* by Noor van Haaften (Christian Focus) includes Joseph in five character studies.

1. Happy families?
(Genesis 37:1–11)

Focus on the **family**

1. **An unwise father and an immature son**
    - Jacob's **favouritism** – he failed to learn from past experience
    - Joseph's **potential** – but he needed experience (and adversity) to mature him

2. **The perfect father and the obedient son**
    - the **Fatherhood** of God (Matthew 7:7–12; Ephesians 3:14–15)
    - Jesus the **Son** and his **Father** (see John's Gospel)

The **obedience of Jesus** – through suffering (Hebrews 5:7–9)

3. **Sons and daughters, brothers and sisters**

    - brought into **God's family** (Galatians 3:26–29)

    - through **Jesus** (Hebrews 2:9–13)

Do you **belong?** Have you **received him?** (John 1:10–13)

2. The green-eyed monster
(Genesis 37:11)

Jealousy and **envy** – deadly diseases

1. **Jealousy – A problem for the brothers**

    • provocation (v. 3)

    • reaction (vv. 4, 8, 11)

    • consequence (vv. 12–36)

2. **Jealousy – A problem for everyone**

    • for the **non–Christian** (Matthew 20:15; Mark 7:21–22)

    • for the **Christian** (1 Corinthians 10:22; Galatians 5:24–26)

Three steps to deal with jealousy:

    • recognition (John 21:21–22; 1 Peter 2:1; Numbers 5:11–31)

    • reassurance (Luke 12:48; Philippians 4:11–13)

    • repentance (1 John 1:9)

3. Anatomy of a crime
(Genesis 37:12–36)

How could such a thing **happen within God's chosen family?**

1. Temptation
'When they saw him in the distance...' (v. 18)

- they were **vulnerable** because seeds of jealousy and hatred had been sown in their minds (Genesis 37:4–5, 8)

- the **importance of the mind** – Matthew 5:21,28; Philippians 4:8, Colossians 3:2)

2. Action
'They stripped him..took him and threw him...' (vv. 23–24)

- the **end–product** – see James 1:13–15; Genesis 3:1–6

- the **only way of escape** : Romans 7:21–25, 8:9–14

3. Consequences
- for the **brothers**: cover–up and deceit
- for **Jacob**: bitter sorrow
- for **Joseph**: utter confusion?

A **far greater example** :the **suffering and death of Jesus** (see Matthew 27:39–44, Isaiah 53:10)

Romans 8:28, 38–39: **your** conviction?

4. Just say 'No'
(Genesis 39)

'The Lord was with Joseph' – **preparing him through testing.**

12 reasons why Joseph **could have said 'yes'**

A **strategy for overcoming sexual temptation :**

1. He refused

2. He gave his reasons

3. He avoided the place of temptation

4. He ran

The **end result: imprisonment**
Compare this with **David**: 2 Samuel 11–12

A message of

- **encouragement** for those who are **tempted :**
  1 Corinthians 10:13; Hebrews 4:15–16; 2 Peter 1:3

- **warning** to those who are **complacent :**
  1 Corinthians 10:12; Matthew 5:27–28

- **hope** for those who have **sinned :**
  1 John 1:9; 2 Corinthians 7:10

5. When God seems to forget
(Genesis 40)

'He forgot him' (v. 23) – Joseph's **lowest point?**

Three reasons why God sometimes **seems to forget**

1. **For the maturing of our character**
    See Romans 5:1–5
    vv. 14–15 – a lesson **still to learn?**
    (see Zechariah 4:6; Romans 12:19; 1 Peter 2:23)

2. **For the strenghtening of our faith**
    Compare Joseph with **Jacob**   (and Thomas – John 20:29)
    See 1 Peter 1:6–9

3. **For the perfecting of his plans**
    'When **two full years** *had passed'* (Genesis 41:1)

He was **right about the means** but **wrong about the timing**

The example of Jesus

- Galatians 4:4–5

- Hebrews 5:7–9

- Matthew 27:46

- Hebrews 12:2

6. From prison to palace
(Genesis 41:1–32)

God's **special day** for Joseph

Three main characters in the story:

1. Pharaoh   – A man who was troubled

God is at work in the life of Pharaoh in order to fulfil his plans.

2. The cupbearer – A man who was reminded

A poor 'witness' – but still used by God.

3. Joseph – A man who was prepared

The lesson Joseph learned through hard experience –
'I cannot ...but God will' (v. 16; see also vv. 25,28 & 32)

The same lesson throughout the Bible:

* prophetic   : Zechariah 4:6
* apostolic   : Philippians 4:12–13
* **Jesus**   : John 15:5

'I cannot but God will' :a lesson for

* the Christian facing adversity
* the non-Christian
* the *'prodigal'* Christian

7. A Spirit-filled man
(Genesis 41:33–40)

Pharaoh recognised in Joseph a man *'in whom is the spirit of God'* (v. 38).

Three characteristics (compare Isaiah 11:2) :

1. Dependence

Joseph acknowledges his entire dependence on God – see vv. 15–16, 25, 28, 32 and compare v. 39.

The peril of prosperity – Deuteronomy 6:10–12.

Characteristic of **the Holy Spirit** (John 16:13–15), and also of **the Lord Jesus Christ** (John 8:28–29).

2. Authority

Joseph's interpretation carried **self–authenticating authority.**

Compare
- **Jesus** (Mark 1:22),
- **his disciples** (Matthew 28:18–20; e.g. 1 Thessalonians 1:4–5)
- **authentic gospel preaching** (1 Corinthians 2:1–5).

3. Wisdom

Not just **explanation** (vv. 25–32) but also **application** (vv. 33–36).
Matthew 7:24–29 : the *'wise man'* hears **and obeys.**

Have **you**?

8. God at work
(Genesis 41:41–57)

God **has been at work** through all Joseph's **adversity**.
God is **still at work** in Joseph's **prosperity** :

1. Promoted by God (vv. 41– 44)

Pharaoh only the **means** – see 45:10; 1 Peter 5:6.

Living with **no regrets or complaints**: Philippians 4:11–13.

2. Prepared by God (vv. 46–49)

- **receiving** God's Word
- **acting** on God's Word

Compare **Noah** – Hebrews 11:7.

Are you prepared? (2 Peter 3)

3. Blessed by God (vv. 45, 50–52)

- a wife
- two sons

Compensation – Mark 10:29–30
Commitment   – Matthew 6:33

4. Vindicated by God   (vv. 53–57)

'Just as Joseph had said' – just as **God** had said (Luke 21:33)
Contrast the **final vindication** – Matthew 25:1–13
Hebrews 2:3: an **unanswerable question**

9. The awakening of conscience
(Genesis 42)

God begins the process by which the brothers' guilty secret is exposed:

1. Natural Disaster
'The famine was severe in the land' (41:57)
God uses the famine to get the brothers to **Egypt.**

2. Harsh Treatment
'Joseph spoke harshly to them' (42:7)
A necessary stage before any real repentance and reconciliation.

3. Troubled Memories
'Surely we are being punished because of our brother' (v. 21)
Fear and **guilt** come to the surface.

4. Unsettling circumstances
'What is this that God has done to us?' (v. 28)
The realisation that **God is the author** of all their circumstances.

Conclusion :

What about *'the perfect crime'?*
Jesus the **Judge** (Romans 2:16) or Jesus the **Saviour** (Hebrews 9:27–28)
Forgiveness available : Psalm 51:1–12; 1 John 2:1–2

10. Mercy withheld
(Genesis 43)

Why does Joseph *'pretend to be a stranger'* (42:7) and not reveal himself to his brothers?

God still has work to do – in the **brothers** and in **Jacob**

1. Jacob: In the cul–de–sac of self-pity

- critical
- insensitive
- pessimistic
- irrational

The only way out – forced to let Benjamin go.

2. The brothers: on the road to repentance

More than just feeling sorry or guilty.
The process which will lead to true repentance continues

- fear (vv. 16–18)
- confusion (vv. 19–23)
- amazement (vv. 26–34)

JOSEPH hides and **weeps** (v. 30) – **God's mercy** withheld

John 11: **the presence of Jesus** withheld

Romans 8:18–27 : **future blessing withheld**

11. The ultimate test
(Genesis 44)

Three stages on the road to repentance for the brothers:

STAGE 1 – Admission (Genesis 42)

'Surely we are being punished because of our brother...' (v. 21)

STAGE 2 – Promise (Genesis 43)

'I myself will guarantee his safety...' (v. 9)

STAGE 3 – Action (Genesis 44)

'..let your servant remain here...in place of the boy...' (v. 33)

Application

Beyond selfishness to **total and unreserved commitment.**

• John 6:53–71

• Luke 9:23–27

• Philippians 3:7–11

Have you **taken and passed the test?**

12. Standing in the gap
(Genesis 44:14–34)

Judah is willing to *'stand in the gap'* (Ezekiel 22:30) for Benjamin. His appeal to Joseph demonstrates **four aspects of intercessory prayer**:

1. The grounds of intercessory prayer

- mercy alone, no merits (compare Luke 18:9–14)
- no bitterness (see Mark 11:25; Psalm 68:19)

2. The content of intercessory prayer

- reciting the facts
- personal and specific

3. The cost of intercessory prayer

- pain, vulnerability
- willingness to offer himself

4. The result of intercessory prayer

- reconciliation
- all the wealth of Egypt

The greatest example: the **Lord Jesus Christ** in his death *'stood in the gap'* for us.

Now he *'always lives to intercede for us'* (Hebrews 7:25)

WANTED! **God is looking for intercessors** who will *'stand in the gap'*

Am I willing?

13. Reconciled!
(Genesis 45)

Reconciliation – at the heart of God

1. The timing of reconciliation

A restored relationship between two parties;

- Joseph, who had forgiven
- the brothers, who were repentant

Two requirements:

- what we must **do**: *'forgive from the heart'*
- what we must **try to do**: *'be reconciled with your brother'*

2. The nature of reconciliation

Judah gets more than he bargained for.
Grace instead of law.

Two necessities:

- *'I am Joseph'* (revealing Jesus)
- *'Do not be distressed'* (full forgiveness)

3. The results of reconciliation

- wonderful joy (Luke 15:7, 10)
- restored as brothers (Romans 8:15–17; Hebrews 2:11)
- all we need (Romans 8:31–32)

'Be reconciled to God' (2 Corinthians 5 :20)

14. Good news of great joy
(Genesis 45:8 – 46:4)

'Joseph is alive!' – good news of great joy **to be shared** (Luke 2:10, 15)

1. Unusual ambassadors

The news carried by **forgiven men** (2 Corinthians 4:7, 5:20)

- their **role:**   to go and tell

- their **message:** Joseph is alive   (compare Luke 24:34)
                          God has made him lord   (compare Acts 2:36)

- their **attitude:**   harmony (45:24)

2. Unexpected news

Jacob has been **living for 22 years**

- under a false premise (37:33)
- which has affected his whole life (37:35)

God finally **vindicates his word** (37:11) and Jacob is convinced (45:28)

3. Unfailing promises

Jacob sets out to Beersheba (see 26:23–24) and experiences

- renewed **fellowship** with God (Hebrews 13:5)
- renewed **promises** from God   (Philippians 1:6)

15. Complete forgiveness
(Genesis 50)

The brothers **fear revenge.**
'Joseph weeps' – and **explains his forgiveness** (vv. 19–21).

1. The present: *'Don't be afraid. Am I in the place of God?'*

Do not *'play God'* – see Romans 12:19–21.
'Fear not' – the message of the gospel – see 1 John 4:16–19.

2. The past: *'You intended to harm me, but God intended it for good to accomplish what is now being done, the saving of many lives.'*

- man's intention – see Matthew 5:21–30.

- God's power – see Acts 2:22–24.

    Isaiah 53:10–12 – God's purpose in salvation.

3. The future: *'So, then, don't be afraid. I will provide for you and your children.'*

A **secure future**: Romans 8:1, 31–39.

Hebrews 11:22 – **Joseph's obituary**

Conclusion:

God's Word – the **antidote to fear.**

Repeated again to the brothers (Compare 45:4–9 with 50:19–21).

An **unforgiving heart** and a **desire for revenge** will **mar the joy of salvation**

8

Loved with everlasting love
(Psalm 107)

The Book of Psalms, the Hebrew hymn-book, is a wonderful resource for both the individual and the people of God, reflecting as it does the whole range of human experience and emotions.

This series of seven is based on one particular Psalm – Psalm 107. Written in beautiful poetry it contains four cameos of need in each of which the Lord answers the cry for help of his people and transforms their situation.

For the titles of each of the seven messages (and the series itself), I chose the opening line of a familiar hymn (which we then sang as part of the service).

The four messages on the specific cameos were revised and given as a weekly series on Radio Scotland.

There is a wealth of written material on the Psalms. In particular, the two-volume Tyndale Commentary by Derek Kidner (IVP 1975) is a masterpiece of succinct and helpful material. At the opposite end of the spectrum (in size) is C. H. Spurgeon's magnus opus – *The Treasury of David'*, reprinted in three volumes by Macdonald Publishing Company, USA. Also older but helpful and reprinted by The Banner of Truth are full commentaries on the Psalms by David Dickson (1959 – first published in 1653–5) and W. S. Plumer (1975 – first published in 1867) and *Psalms* by Alan Harman (Christian Focus) and *Prayer, Praise and Prophecy* by Geoffrey Grogan (Mentor).

1. There is a redeemer
(Psalm 107:1–3)

The **theme** of the Psalm – *'Give thanks to the Lord'*

1. **The people who should give thanks to the Lord**

    •   the redeemed (see 1 Peter 1:18–20)

    •   from everywhere (see Revelation 14:3)

2. **The reason they should give thanks to the Lord**

    •   for his goodness to his people

    •   for his redemption of his people from

        —   hunger and thirst (vv. 4–9)

        —   captivity and slavery (vv. 10–16)

        —   sickness and death (vv. 17–22)

        —   danger and despair (vv. 23–32)

    •   for his transforming power

        —   from prosperity to adversity

        —   from adversity to prosperity

So, **the wise** should **consider the great love of the Lord** (v. 43) and **give thanks to him in all situations** (vv. 8, 15, 21, 31)

2. Guide me, O Thou great Jehovah
(Psalm 107:4–9)

Transformed circumstances

1. **Dying in the Desert** (vv. 4–6a)

    Deep distress:

    • **disorientation** – *'wandering in desert wastelands'*

    • **dissatisfaction** – *'hungry and thirsty'*

    • **desperation** – *'their lives ebbed away'*

    A **cry for help** to the Lord

2. **Celebrating in the City** (vv. 6b–9)

    Dramatic deliverance

    • **direction** – *'he led them by a straight way'*
      See John 14:6; Matthew 7:13–14

    • **destination** – *'a city where they could settle'*
      See Hebrews 12:22–24; Revelation 21–22

    • **declaration** – *'he satisfies the thirsty and fills the hungry with good things'*
      See Luke 1:46–55; John 6:35

    A **song of thanksgiving** to the Lord

3. Out of my bondage, my sorrow and night
(Psalm 107:10–16)

Another picture (compare vv. 4–9) of **transformed circumstances** – the **release of prisoners**

1. **Rebellion (vv. 10–13a)**
   The **consequences of rejecting God's authority** (v. 11)
   - **shackled in a dark dungeon**
     - — slavery
     - — misery
   - **sentenced to hard labour**
     - — damaging the body
     - — breaking the spirit
   - **sprawled at death's door**
     - — no strength
     - — no help

   '**Then** *they cried to the Lord...*'

2. **Rescue (vv. 13b–16)**
   A **speedy and effective answer**
   - **light**
     - — joy, instead of despair
     - — hope, instead of fear

   See Luke 1:78–79; Luke 2:32; Hebrews 2:14–15
   - **liberty**
     - — personal
     - — total

   See Romans 6:1–14

'*Let them* **give thanks** *to the Lord...*'

4. Come, ye sinners, poor and needy, wounded, weak and sore
(Psalm 107:17–22)

From the **desert** (vv. 4–9) to the **prison** (vv. 10–16) to the *'hospital'* (vv. 17–22)

1. The Patient and his Problem (vv. 17–19a)

The *'fool'* and his *'affliction'*
- **its cause** – self–inflicted
  see Deuteronomy 28:58–61, but note John 9:1–2
- **its symptoms** – loss of appetite
  compare Job 33:19–22
- **its prognosis** – *'the gates of death'*
  see Romans 6:23

2. The Physician and his Remedy (vv. 19b–22)

The **Lord** and his **salvation**
- **the means** of salvation – *'he sent forth his word'*
  — the **word** of the Lord – Genesis 1:3; Hebrews 1:1
  — the **Word** – John 1:14; Hebrews 1:2
- **the effects** of salvation
  — restoration to health (Isaiah 53:4–6)
  — rescue from death (1 Corinthians 15:55–57)
- **the outcome** of salvation
  — praise
  — witness
  see Hebrews 13:15–16

5. Eternal Father, strong to save
(Psalm 107:23–32)

A journey at sea – through crisis to safety

1. Wit's End (vv. 23–28a)

    Unexpected circumstances
    *   out on the sea
        — legitimate business
        — necessary for work
    *   out of control
        — mind and emotions
        — body
    The purpose – *'then they cried out to the Lord'* (see Jonah 1)

2. Journey's End (vv. 28b–32)

    The Lord's response
    *   out of distress
        — peace
        — joy
    The lesson – Mark 4:35–41
    *   out of danger
        — the *'desired haven'* (see John 14:1–3)
        — *'no more sea'* (Revelation 21:1–4)

The result : *'let them give thanks'* – praise and witness

6. Teach me thy way, O Lord
(Psalm 107:43)

The way of wisdom – *'consider the **great love** of the Lord'*

1.   In History

The length of the Lord's unfailing love – **shown to Israel**:
- Psalm 105 – from Abraham to deliverance from Egypt
- Psalm 106 – from the Red Sea to Canaan to exile
- Psalm 107 – return from captivity

The **climax** of human history – Galatians 4:4–5; Romans 5:8

2.   In Extremity

The depths of the Lord's unfailing love – **shown in human need**:
- the **lost** – dying in the desert (vv. 4–9)
- the **prisoner** – helpless in the dungeon (vv. 10–16)
- the **sick** – at death's door (vv. 17–22)
- the **storm–tossed** – at his wits' end (vv. 23–32)
- the **hungry** – in the barren desert (vv. 33–38)
- the **oppressed** – facing a hostile enemy (vv. 39–41)

The **Lord's salvation** – seen supremely in **the cross** (1 John 4:10)

3.   In Eternity

The extent of the Lord's unfailing love – **shown by the redeemed**:
- on **earth** (vv. 1–2, 8–9, 15–16, 21–22, 31–32, 42)
- in **heaven** (Revelation 1:5, 5:9–14)

9

The radical teaching of Jesus
(Luke 12–13)

It is difficult for us to grasp just how radical the teaching of Jesus was – especially if we have been inoculated against it by over-familiarity. A more fundamental problem which confronts us is that, unless we are conversant with the current teaching and practices of first-century Judaism, we will miss the shocking impact of what Jesus taught – so revolutionary that in the end the religious leadership of Israel decided to silence him.

For example, if we say *'Samaritan',* most people think 'good Samaritan'. But, for a first century Jew the words 'good' and 'Samaritan' never went together – only 'bad Samaritan'. And that is why Jesus' parable about a 'good Samaritan' was so surprising, even offensive to his hearers.

Similarly, the word *'Pharisee'* which the dictionary defines as follows: **Pharisee** *n. 1. a member of an ancient Jewish sect teaching strict observance of Jewish traditions. 2. a self-righteous or hypocritical person.*

At the time when Jesus spoke, **only definition 1 applied** – the Pharisees were a strict and orthodox Jewish religious group who tried to obey the law of Moses in every detail. It is only because of the teaching of Jesus that the second definition came into force. But at the time of Jesus, **everyone** looked up to the Pharisees and respected them as people at the pinnacle of religious life, as those closest to God. Imagine the shock then, as Jesus stands up and publicly denounces them as 'snakes', 'whitewashed graves', 'blind guides', 'a brood of vipers', 'hypocrites' and murderers.

In Luke chapters 12 and 13, we have the record of a series of challenges which Jesus presents – not just to the people (and especially religious people) of his day, but also to us in our day. I have tried to bring home the contemporary challenge by giving a title to each in the form of a question.

Standard commentaries on Luke as recommended before will provide the necessary exegesis. I am not aware of any books devoted solely to these specific chapters.

1. Are you a hypocrite?
(Luke 12:1–3)

A warning about **three aspects of hypocrisy**

1.   **The DECEIT of hypocrisy**

  •   an **actor** – the real self hidden behind the mask
  (see Matthew 23:25–28)

  •   the problem of **self–deceit** – the act becomes the reality
  (see Jeremiah 17:9; Hosea 7:9; Revelation 3:17)

2.   **THE DANGER of hypocrisy**

  Hypocrisy is **like yeast**

  •   small in proportion to the whole

  •   unobtrusive and gradual in its effects

  •   finally taking over completely

3.   **THE DISCLOSURE of hypocrisy**

  One day all pretence will be **exposed**; every secret **made public**

  •   the day of **judgement to come** (Romans 2:16; Acts 17:31)
  •   the day of **salvation now** (John 3:16–19)

The ANTIDOTE to hypocrisy – radical change
*'You must be **born again**'* (John 3:7; 2 Corinthians 5:17)

2. Are you afraid?
(Luke 12:4–12)

FEAR : an intruder in God's world (Genesis 3:10).
Jesus **addresses the fears** of his followers (*'my friends'*)

1. The fear of BEING KILLED (verses 4–5)
Growing opposition to Jesus may lead to **violent death** but

- there is more to life than the body : the *'soul'*
- there is a fate worse than death : *'hell'*
- there is a greater power than human authority : God

So, *'Fear him..Yes, I tell you, fear him....'* (verse 5)

2. The fear of BEING FORGOTTEN (verses 6–7)
Look at **God's care** for

- the sparrow : insignificant creatures
- the hairs of your head : smallest details

'You are worth more..'

3. The fear of BEING DISOWNED (verses 8–10)

- the **present** (*'before men'*) is the key to the **future** (*'before the angels of God'*)
- **the unforgivable sin** : rejecting the Holy Spirit's witness

Assurance : Romans 10: 9

4. The fear of BEING UNABLE TO COPE (verses 11–12)
In **unexpected circumstances**

- a *'defence counsel'* is promised (see Acts 4:8–22)

3. Are you rich?
(Luke 12:13–21)

The man in the crowd : concerned with the **trivial** (verse 13) instead of the **important** (verse 14).

The danger of **greed/covetousness** (verse 15) illustrated with **a parable**:

1.   THE RICH MAN WHO WAS A FOOL (verses 16–20)

His plans seemed **wise,** but in God's eyes he was **a fool** because he was **concerned only with**

- the **material** (instead of the **spiritual**)

- the **temporal** (instead of the **eternal**)

- **himself** (instead of **God**)

At **death** (too late) he discovered he was **a fool.**

2.   THE FOOL WHO IS RICH (verse 21)

All of us are **paupers** so far as God is concerned (Ephesians 2:1–3),
     'but God...'

- *'rich **in mercy**'* (Ephesians 2:4)

- rich **through Jesus** (2 Corinthians 8:9)

- **grace** through faith (Ephesians 2;8–9)

We are *'fools for Christ'* (1 Corinthians 4:10–13) but are *'rich towards God'* with *' treasure in heaven'* (verse 33).

THE FINAL VERDICT :   *'Well done!'* or *'You fool!'* ?

4. Are you worried?
(Luke 12:22–34)

Jesus turns from the problem of **greed** (verse 15) to that of **worry**.

NEGATIVE – *'Do not worry'* (verse 22)

- **practical** – worry is a waste of time and effort.

- **personal** – we have a God who is the

  — *Provider* (*'ravens'* & *'lilies'*)

  — *Father* (Luke 11:2–4)

  — *Shepherd* (*'little flock'*)

POSITIVE – *'Seek his kingdom'* (verse 31)

- **we belong** to a different kingdom, so we

- **seek its interests** first and foremost, and

- **hold on lightly** to material things

THE PROMISE:

- on **earth** – God will provide

- in **heaven** – treasure

So, **why worry?**

5. Are you ready?
(Luke 12:35 – 48)

Jesus warns his disciples to **be ready** for his return, by means of **two linked parables.**

1. **THE MASTER'S RETURN**

   - it is *'late'* (verse 45; 2 Peter 3)

   - it is **unexpected** (verse 40; 1 Thessalonians 5)

2. **THE SERVANT'S READINESS**

   'Watching' (verse 37) and *'doing'* (verse 43)

   - personal preparation (verse 35; see Hebrews 12:1)

   - active witness (verse 35; see Matthew 5:14–15)

   - responsible service (verse 42; see Matt. 25:31–46)

3. **THE FINAL RECKONING**

   Criteria for judgement (verses 47–48) :
   - knowledge (see Matthew 10:15, 11:22–24)

   - *'gifting'* (see Matthew 25:14–30)

'The judgement seat of Christ' – 2 Corinthians 5:10

So, **be prepared!**

6. Are you wise?
(Luke 12:49–59)

Jesus asks **three questions** which show that the people, and even the disciples, **failed to understand** what he is teaching:

1. *'Do you think I came to bring peace on earth?'*
    Are you wise about THE MINISTRY OF JESUS? **(verses 49–53)**

    - *'distressed'*
    - *'a baptism'*
    - *'fire'*

    Division caused by the response of the hearers.
    The cost for the disciple (see Matthew 10: 32–39)

2. *'How is it that you don't know how to interpret this present time?'*
    Are you wise about THE TIMES WE LIVE IN? **(verses 54–56)**

    'Hypocrites' – play–acting with trivialities. A **danger** for

    - the **non–Christian** (compare verses 16–21).
    - the **Christian** (see Ephesians 5:15–16, Colossians 4:5–6)

3. *'Why don't you judge for yourselves what is right?'*
    Are you wise about THE JUDGEMENT THAT IS COMING? **(verses 57–59)**

    - settle out of court **now** or
    - face the penalty **then.**

    'Be reconciled to God' – the price has been paid
    (see 2 Corinthians 5:16–21)

7. Are you guilty?
(Luke 13:1–5)

Jesus counteracts wrong views about tragedy (compare the Book of Job; John 9:1–2) with **general lessons for everyone:**

1. ALL ARE SINNERS

- no direct correlation between sin and suffering (see Psalm 130:3)

- no–one is innocent before God (Romans 3:9–12)

2. ALL WILL PERISH

- the wages of sin : Romans 6:23

- more than physical death (see 12:4–5)

3. UNLESS YOU REPENT

- a change of mind towards God (Acts 20:21)

- the message of Jesus – Mark 1:15

- the reason for the coming of Jesus : John 3:16

CONCLUSIONS

- God **uses tragedy** to wake us up.

- **no tragedy** – only triumph for the Christian (Philippians 1:21)

8. Are you fruitful?
(Luke 13:6–9)

Fruitfulness – the proof of obedience to God's Word.

1. The CARE of the owner

- Israel (Isaiah 5:1–7)

- the Church

2. The COMING of the owner

- again and again

- finally, in judgement

3. The COMPLAINT of the owner

- nothing at all?

- nothing but leaves?

4. The COMMAND of the owner

- unless we remain in Christ (John 15:5–6)

- more evidence – less excuse (see Matthew 11:20–24)

5. The COMPASSION of the owner

- too late for Israel (Matthew 21:18–19; Luke 23:27–31)

- still time for us? (2 Peter 3:9)

10

Songs for Pilgrims
(Psalm 120–134)

There have been some interesting and significant shifts of emphasis in recent times in how Christians describe and explain their faith. Whereas once the focus was on the need for a crisis conversion experience (making it almost mandatory to be able to name the time and the place), the process of coming to faith is now a more dominant theme and the motif of the Christian life as a journey has been suggested as more appealing to our post-modern generation.

These emphases are not mutually exclusive and both can find Scriptural warrant. The idea of a journey or pilgrimage finds echoes in the wilderness wanderings of the people of Israel en route from Egypt to the Promised Land, let alone more recently with Bunyan's classic 'Pilgrim's Progress'.

In an age where travel was mostly on foot (and consequently much slower) there was time for reflection – not only on the ultimate destination but also on the journey itself and the lessons that the pilgrims learned through their journeying experiences.

One section of the Psalter (the fifteen Psalms from 120 to 134 inclusive) is believed by many to be a collection of songs for or by pilgrims en route from their homes (even from distant 'Meshech' and 'Kedar' in the opening psalm) to the temple in Jerusalem for one of the major festivals around which the annual cycle of the lives of the Israelites revolved. Some even suggest they were sung as the priests and people ascended the steps into the temple itself (with a psalm on each of fifteen steps!)

As with all the Psalms, these songs can also be sung by Christians today for we share similar experiences and aspirations as we journey towards 'the heavenly Jerusalem, the city of the living God' (Hebrews 12: 22). Our ultimate goal is not just the city but, as the last book of the Bible tells us, the one who is its light and life – the Lord Jesus Christ, the Lamb of God.

In addition to the recommended books on the Psalms given under the series 'Loved with Everlasting Love', I have found two other books on these specific psalms to be most helpful:

The Journey (A Guide Book for the Pilgrim Life) by Eugene H. Peterson, Marshall Pickering, 1995.

Higher Ground (Insights from the Psalms of Ascent) by R. T. Kendall, Christian Focus, 1995.

1. 'In my distress'
(Psalm 120)

'Woe is me!' – the **lowest point** from which the **journey begins**

1. **The reason for the psalmist's distress**

    Living in a **'war–zone'**
    *   the **people**
        *   *'Meshech'* (Ezekiel 32:26)
        *   *'Kedar'* (Isaiah 21:16–17)
    *   the **weapons**
        *   *'lying lips'*
        *   *'deceitful tongues'*

The **lie** (Gen. 3:4–5; Jn 8:44) and the **reality** (Rom. 3:9–18)

2. **The result of the psalmist's distress**

    He **'calls on the Lord'** who **'answers'** in
    *   **salvation** – from a false way of life (Ephesians 2:1–3)
        *   Abraham (Genesis 12:1–4; Hebrews 11:8–10)
        *   the Christian (1 Peter 1:18–21; 2:11–12)
    *   **judgement**
        *   not retaliation (Romans 12:17–21)
        *   in kind (verses 3–4)

    The **way of Christ** – 1 Peter 2:21–25

2. 'Where does my help come from?'
(Psalm 121)

A search for **security in life**

1. **POTENTIAL PROBLEMS**

   Three dangers on the journey:

   - the slip (verse 3)
   - the sun (verse 6a)
   - the moon (verse 6b)

   No hope from *'the hills'* (verse 1)

2. **PROMISED PROTECTION**

   The assurance of **help from God** that is

   - **powerful** (verse 2)
     - the Creator (contrast Romans 1:20–25)
     - the Lord (Isaiah 44:6–20: Psalm 95:3–7)
   - **personal**
     - *'shade'* (verse 5)
     - *'keeper'* (verses 3, 4, 5, 7, 8)
   - **perpetual**
     - *'neither slumber nor sleep'* (verses 3–4)
     - *'coming and going'* (verse 8a)
     - *'now and for evermore'* (verse 8b)

   The promise : *'kept from all **evil**'* (verse 7; Romans 8:28–39)

3. 'Let us go to the house of the Lord'
(Psalm 122)

The joyful pilgrim **arrives for worship**

1. **THE PLACE OF WORSHIP**

    The *'house of the Lord'* (verses 2–3)

    *   the *'heavenly Jerusalem'* (Hebrews 12:22–24)
    *   *'neither on this mountain nor in Jerusalem'* (John 4:21–24)

    Wherever Christians meet (e.g. 1 Cor. 1:2; Galatians 1:2)

2. **THE PEOPLE OF WORSHIP**

    The *'tribes of Israel'* (verse 4)

    *   encouragement (verse 1; Hebrews 10:24–25)
    *   edification (verse 3; Ephesians 2:19–22)

    People from *'every tribe'* (Revelation 14:6; Matthew 24:14)

3. **THE PURPOSE OF WORSHIP**

    *   **praise** (verse 4)
        *   *'decreed'* (verse 4; Psalm 136:1–3)
        *   *'judgement'* (verse 5; John 5:26–27)
    *   **prayer** – for *'Jerusalem'* (verses 6–9)
        *   peace (contrast Luke 19:41–44)
        *   prosperity (Matthew 5:14–16)

    Final fulfilment (Revelation 21)

4. 'I lift up my eyes to you'
(Psalm 123)

The upward look – three aspects of a relationship with God

1.   THE SUBJECT & HIS KING (verse 1)
Submission to God
• on earth (Psalm 122:5)
• in heaven (Isaiah 66:1–2)
The example of Jesus – Hebrews 5:7–8)

2.   THE SLAVE & HIS MASTER (verse 2)
Service for God
• waiting for instructions
• belonging to God (Romans 12:1–2)
The example of Jesus – John 13:12–17

3.   THE SUPPLICANT & HIS LORD (verses 3–4)
Salvation from God
• *'much contempt'* and *'much ridicule'*
• from *'the proud'* and *'the arrogant'*
The example of Jesus – Hebrews 12:1–2

The downward look – God's love seen in
• the **condescension** of Jesus (Philippians 2:6–8)
• the **exaltation** of Jesus (Philippians 2:9–11)
Mercy and grace *'from the throne'* (Hebrews 4:14–16)

5. 'If the Lord had not been on our side'
(Psalm 124)

'If the Lord had not been...' (verses 1–2) –
the experience of God's people – past and present.

1. **LIFE–THREATENING HAZARDS**
   Four pictures of enemy action

   • the **fearsome monster** (verse 3)
     — small and insignificant
     — *'swallowed alive'*

   • the **flash flood** (verses 4–5)
     — sudden and unexpected
     — *'swept away'*

   • the **fierce animal** (verse 6)
     — slow and painful
     — *'torn by their teeth'*

   • the **fowler's snare** (verse 7)
     — trapped and struggling
     — strangling

2. **LIFE–SAVING HELP**
   Our help (verse 8)

   • *'the name of the Lord'* – his **character**
     — the love of God (John 3:16)
     — *'Jesus'* (Matthew 1:21)

   • *'the Maker of heaven and earth'* – his **power**
     — the cross (Colossians 2:15)
     — the resurrection (1 Corinthians 15:20–28, 50–58)
   'If God be for us....?' – Romans 8:28–39

6. 'The Lord surrounds his people'
(Psalm 125)

As you look out from the city...

...**what do you see?**

1. **A city surrounded by God? (verses 1–2)**
   - those who trust in the LORD....

     cannot be shaken
   - true security   (John 13:3–4)

2. **A CITY RULED BY THE WICKED? (verses 3–4)**
   - bad things happen to good people
   - so
     - count the cost (Luke 14:25–33)
     - don't envy the wicked (Psalm 93:1–3, 12–17)
     - persevere – it won't last! (1 Cor. 10:13)
     - pray for the good (Romans 8:28–29;
       Ecclesiastes 7:29)

3. **A CITY WITHOUT JUSTICE?   (verse 5)**
   - there will come a day (Hebrews 9:27)
   - no wrong turns! (Galatians 5:7; Job 23:11)
     - it's not fair? (Matthew 20:1–16)

Peace = trust

7. 'Restore our fortunes ,O Lord'
(Psalm 126)

Present problems which cause the Psalmist to **look back** and **look forward**

1. **LOOKING BACK – SONGS OF JOY RECALLED (verses 1–3)**

   A **complete transformation** of circumstances
   * unexpected and unbelievable (see Acts 12:1–19)
   * joy and laughter (contrast Psalm 137:1–6)
   * praise to the Lord
     — from the nations
     — from his people

   Past experience produces **hope for the future**

2. **LOOKING FORWARD – SONGS OF JOY RESTORED (verses 4–6)**

   A **prayer for help**
   * **divine intervention** (verse 4)
     — sudden and powerful
     — life–giving
   * **human endeavour** (verses 5–6)
     — going out and coming home
     — seed and sheaves
     — tears and joy

   Only God gives growth (1 Corinthians 3:5–7)

The Lord's **final intervention** – Matthew 13:36–43; James 5:7–8

8. 'In vain?'
(Psalm 127)

Human preoccupations –
- building (verse 1)
- security (verse 2)
- family (verses 3–5)

Is it all *'in vain'*?   (Ecclesiastes 1–3)

1.   Human activity WITHOUT THE LORD is FRUITLESS (verses 1–2) *'Unless the Lord'*
- *'builds the house'*
- *'watches over the city'*

Then, no matter how hard you work (Genesis 3:17–19), it is all **a waste of time** (Luke 12:16–20; John 15:5; 1 Cor. 3:10–15)

2.   Human activity WITH THE LORD is FRUITFUL (verses 3–5)

An example – **the gift of children**
- *'reward'* &
- responsibility (Genesis 1:28)

Other *'children'* (Hebrews 2:10; 3 John 4)

A WARNING – **Solomon** (1 Kings 11:1–13)

A BLESSING – **sleep** (verse 2; Luke 8:23; Acts 12:6)

9. 'Blessings and prosperity will be yours'
(Psalm 128)

The *'health and wealth gospel'*? (contrast Psalm 73, 129)

1.   **A PRINCIPLE (verse 1)**

'Blessing' (happiness) for those who

• *'fear the Lord'* – **reverence** (Hebrews 12:28–29)

• *'walk in his ways'* – **obedience** (Deuteronomy 8:6)

To **do otherwise** is pointless – and **painful!** (Acts 26:14)

2.   **A PROMISE (verses 2–4)**

God's purpose – **fruitfulness** (Genesis 1:27–31) seen in

• satisfying **work**

• productive **relationships**

John 4:31–38 – the **most satisfying** *'food'*

3.   **A PRAYER (verses 5–6)**

Future blessings from the Lord

• *'from Zion'* – the Lord's **presence**

• *'of Jerusalem'* – the Lord's **people**

• *'upon Israel'* – the Lord's **peace**

Greater blessings (Hebrews 12:22–24);

eternal life (Revelation 22:1–5)

10. 'But they have not gained the victory over me'
(Psalm 129)

The **song of the suffering people of God**

1.   **The persecution of God's people** (verses 1–2a, 3)
       Oppression from enemies that is
       • **persistent** – from the *'youth'* of
              —   Israel (Exodus 1)
              —   the church (Acts 4)
       • **painful**
              —   the whip
              —   the plough
       'Blessing' – Matthew 5:10–12

2.   **The perseverance of God's people** (verse 2b, 4)
       Undefeated because of
              • the Lord's **character** – *'righteous'*
              • the Lord's **control** – *'he has cut me free...'*
       Final assurance – Jude 24–25

3.   **THE PERSPECTIVE OF GOD'S PEOPLE** (verses 5–8)
       The **fate of those who** *'hate Zion'*
              • no **progress**
              • no **prosperity**
              • no **promise**
       A **passionate concern** – Matthew 6:9–10; 33

The **song of the suffering Son of God?**   (Isaiah 53)

11. 'Out of the depths'
(Psalm 130)

Four rungs on the ladder *'out of the depths of anguish to the heights of assurance'* (Spurgeon)

1.   **DESPERATION** (verses 1–2)
      Seen in
      •   the **place** – *'the depths'*
      •   the **plea** – *'my cry for mercy'*
      Where **everyone must start** (Luke 18:13–14)

2.   **AFFIRMATION** (verses 3–4)
      Based on
      •   God's **justice** – *'who could stand?'* (Romans 3:9–18)
      •   God's **grace** – *'with you there is forgiveness'* (Ex. 34:6–7)
      The **result** – *'therefore you are feared'* (Hebrews 12:28–29)

3.   **EXPECTATION** (verses 5–6)
      Waiting for
      •   the **Lord**
      •   the **morning**
      Certain hope – based on *'his word'* (Romans 15:4)

4.   **ANTICIPATION** (verses 7–8)
      A **greater vision** beyond
      •   **himself** – for *'Israel'* (Malachi 4:1–2; Luke 2:25–38)
      •   **his experience** – *'full redemption'* (Ephesians 1:7–8)
      Fulfilled in Jesus who descended to *'the depths'* (1 Peter 3:18–22)

12. 'Like a weaned child'
(Psalm 131)

A *'weaned child'* – not *'a rebellious runaway or a whining baby'*
(Peterson)

1.   The danger of unbridled ambition (v. 1)

The **rebel** (Genesis 3:1–7; Isaiah 2:12–14) who must be **humbled**

• a right relationship with God (Psalm 130:1–4)

• a right estimate of myself (Romans 12:1–3)

Godly ambition – Philippians 3:12–15

2.   The danger of unhealthy dependency (verse 2)

The **baby** (John 3:3) who must be **weaned**

• maturity (1 Corinthians 3:2; Hebrews 5:12–13)

• the Giver – not his gifts (John 6:25–35)

Ultimate security (Job 1:20–22, 42:1–3)

A plea to others (verse 3)

Fulfilled in Jesus

• his **invitation** – Matthew 11:28–30

• his **illustration** – Matthew 18:1–4

13. 'The Lord swore an oath'
(Psalm 132)

The need for *'bifocal vision'*

1. **TWO OATHS**

   • **David's oath**   (verses 2–9)
   — worship before rest (1 Chronicles 13–16)
   — righteousness and joy   (1 Kings 8:17–19)
   — an unfulfilled oath (1 Chronicles 22:5–10)

   • **the Lord's oath** (verses 11–18)
   — the wrong way round! (1 Chronicles 17:10b–14)
   — the Lord has chosen Zion! (Zechariah 2:10; 8: 2)
   — God keeps his promises! (1 Kings 8:20)

2. **TWO KINGS**

   • **King David** (verse 1)
   — the anointed King   (1 Samuel 16:13)
   — a righteous heart   (1 Kings 3:6)

   • **King of Judah**   (verses 10, 12)
   — *'For the sake of....'* (2 Chronicles 6:40–42)
   — *'If...'*
   — a future hope (Daniel 9:25–26; Rev. 5:5)

3. **ONE MESSIAH** (verses 17–19)

   • the unchangeable Oath (Hebrews 6:13–20)
   • the new dwelling in Zion (John 1:14; Rev. 21:1–4)
   • *'The Lord's anointed'* (Acts 4:25–26; Luke 4:17–21)

14. 'Living together in unity'
(Psalm 133)

Unity is....

1.   **Being part of a family**
      'Brothers live together in unity'   (verse 1)

   •   brothers, not friends (Ephesians 2:14–22)

   •   brothers, not strangers (Psalm 69:8; 1 John 4:19–21)

'In God's family, there is no such thing as an only child'

2.   **Working its way down**
      '..like precious oil' (verse 2)

   •   through the High Priest (Leviticus 21:10; Hebs 4:14–
       5:10)

   •   from the top down (Exodus 29:5–9)

3.   **An overflowing blessing**
      '...as if the dew of Hermon' (verse 3)

   •   fresh and expectant (Psalm 110:2–3)

   •   God's abundant blessing (Deuteronomy 30:15–20; John
       3:36)

Union...Communion

15. Blessings without end
(Psalm 134)

Journey's end – in the temple on Mount Zion

1. **Bless the Lord (verses 1–2)**

   True worship:

   - who? (1 Chronicles 23:30; 1 Peter 2:9)

   - why? (Psalm 103:1–2, 18:30–31; Romans 8:28)

   - how? (Romans 12:1–2)

   - when? (Job 1:20, 2:9–10; Philippians 4:4)

   - where? (1 Chronicles 23:28; Matthew 18:20)

2. **The Lord bless you (verse 3)**

   God's character seen in his blessing

   - his **power** – *'the Lord, the Maker of heaven and earth'* (Jeremiah 32:17)

   - his **love** – *'from Zion'*
     (Hebrews 12:22–24)

Those whom the Lord blesses, **bless the Lord** (Ephesians 1:3–14)

11

A Mission which Changed the World
(Acts 13–14)

A question I like to ask people who are familiar with the Bible is: 'If you had lived in the first century, which of the churches described in the New Testament would you have liked to belong to?'

Not many answer 'Corinth' – and even fewer 'Laodicea' (though this is only with the hindsight of Scripture – most of us would have probably admired this large and wealthy church).

The church I find most attractive and interesting is that described in Acts 11 – the 'International Christian Fellowship' in Antioch, the third city of the Roman Empire (after Rome and Alexandria). It was founded by unnamed believers from Cyprus and Cyrene who took the then radical step of proclaiming the good news about Jews to Greeks and not just Jews.

The first largely Gentile local church soon came to the attention of the church in Jerusalem who wisely sent Barnabas ('son of encouragement') to check what was happening and report back. Finding clear evidence of the grace of God at work in the Antioch church, Barnabas took another wise step and went and brought the ex-Pharisee Saul from his home in Tarsus, some ten years after his dramatic conversion to Christ.

The teaching gifts of Saul/ Paul, and the pastoral gifts of Barnabas combined to great effect to lay strong foundations in the Christian congregation at Antioch where significantly the 'Followers of the Way' were first given the nickname 'Christians'.

Of even greater significance, however, were the seismic shifts in the spread of the gospel that were taking place under the direction of the Holy Spirit – not only from Jews to Gentiles, but also from Jerusalem and Judea and Samaria to the ends of the earth as the Lord Jesus himself had promised (Acts 1:8).

The first ripple spread from the church at Antioch with the commissioning of Barnabas and Saul on the first-ever 'missionary journey'. The rest is history (described in the second half of the Book of Acts and the subsequent history of the first three centuries) but we should not minimise the significance of the events described by Luke in Acts 13 and 14. It was truly 'A mission which changed the world'.

The series begins with the mission-mandate of the Jerusalem church (Acts 1:1–11) and then an introduction to the church at Antioch (Acts 11:19–30, 13:1–3) followed by five sermons on the journey itself (Acts 13:4 – 14:28).

D. A. Carson (New Testament Commentary Survey, IVP, 1993) comments that 'the Book of Acts is still not particularly well-served by commentaries'.

Two commentaries by F. F. Bruce are both helpful. The earlier one in the New London Commentary series (Eerdamns, 1954) is now out of print but has been reprinted by IVP (1991). The original Tyndale New Testament Commentary by E. M. Blaiklock (1959) has now been replaced by an expanded commentary by I. Howard Marshall (1983). Perhaps the best and most thorough on the text is that by Richard N. Longenecker in the Expositor's Bible Commentary (Zondervan, 1995).

Of great value to preachers are the large Bible Speaks Today Commentary by J. R. W. Stott (IVP, 1990) which also contains a useful study guide appendix, and Tom Houston's new book in the *Characters* series, *Characters Around the Church: Witnesses to the birth of the Jerusalem Church*, (Christian Focus). From an American expositor, James Montgomery Boice (Baker, 1997) is a helpful contribution with fifty chapters on the whole book.

1. 'You will be my witnesses'
(Acts 1:1–11)

Three stages in the progress **from disciples to witnesses:**

1.   From the resurrection to the ascension –   *'standing and staring'*
Forty days when Jesus is with the disciples:
>important **evidence**
>important **teaching**
>important **instructions**

Then **Jesus is taken into heaven**

2.   From the ascension to Pentecost – *'sitting and waiting'*
Ten days when the disciples are alone in the upper room
>Jesus has **ascended**
>the Holy Spirit is **not yet given**

The **day of Pentecost** – the promise fulfilled (Acts 1:4–8; 2:1–4)

3.   From Pentecost to the return of Christ – *'going and telling'*
An **indefinite period** for bearing witness
>**explanation** (Acts 2:14–21)
>**proclamation** (Acts 2:22–35)
>**application** (Acts 2:36–40)

The **mission begins** – *'to the ends of the earth'* (Acts 2:5–11)

CHALLENGES for every church and every Christian
>we are **called to witness**
>we are **equipped to witness**

'..to the very end of the age' (Matthew 28:18–20)

2. The church where it began
(Acts 11:19–30, 13:1–3)

The **mandate** (1:8) carried out **through persecution** (8:1)

The **focus shifts**

> from the established *'Jewish'* church in Jerusalem to

> a new *'cosmopolitan'* church in Antioch (see 13:1)

from where the *'mission that changed the world'* is launched

1.   **The beginning of a church (11:19–21)**

The **importance of witnesses** who

- carry the message
- to all people

The **result** – the church **grows**

2.   **The establishing of a church (11:22–26)**

The **importance of**

- **pastors** to encourage the people (Barnabas)
- **teachers** to strengthen the church (Saul)

The **result** – the church **matures**

3.   **The giving of a church (11:27–30, 13:1–3)**

The **importance of** *'prophets'* to stimulate the church **to give**

- **resources** (aid to the church in Jerusalem)
- **people** (Barnabas and Saul)

The **result** – the church **reproduces**

3. Starting in Cyprus
(Acts 13:4–12)

The first **planned missionary enterprise** of the church : An *'idea whose time had come'* (see Galatians 4:4)

1. **Obeying the call of the Lord**
   Saul and Barnabas **sent**

   • by the **church** (verse 3)

   • by the **Spirit** (verse 4)

   Both are necessary

2. **Proclaiming the Word of the Lord**
   A clear **strategy** (see Romans 1:16)

   • to the **Jews** first

   • then to the **Gentiles** (see Acts 26:16–18; Romans 10:1)

   A **powerful message** – from **God**

3. **Facing the enemy of the Lord**
   The **work of the enemy** through human agency

   • to **deceive** : not Bar–Jesus but *'child of the devil'*

   • to **divert** – perversion instead of conversion

   The **end result – faith in Jesus**

4. Preaching in Pisidian Antioch
(Acts 14:13–43)

Verbal proclamation of the message – the **chief activity** of the missionaries.

Authentic preaching – to the **whole person**:

1. A message which ENGAGES THE MIND

   The **focus** of Paul's sermon – **JESUS**

   • the **culmination of history** in Jesus (verses 17–25)

   • the **fulfilment of Scripture** in Jesus (verses 26–37)

   • the **forgiveness of sins** in Jesus (verses 38–42)

2. A message which STIRS THE EMOTIONS

   The **target** of Paul's sermon – his **Jewish audience**

   • through the **content of** the message

   • through the **response to** the message

3. A message which CHALLENGES THE WILL

   The **aim** of Paul's sermon – **faith in Jesus**

   • the **importance of belief**

   • the **danger of unbelief**

The importance of **continuing in the grace of God** (verse 43)
See Galatians 1:6, 3:1–3

5. How the world was changed
(Acts 13:44 – 14:7)

The good news of Jesus – **powerful in its effects** (Romans 1:16)

1. **A message which AROUSES GREAT INTEREST**
   whenever and **wherever** it is proclaimed
   - Jesus (e.g. Matthew 7:28 – 8:1)
   - the apostles (13:44–45, 14:1)
   - **us?**

2. **A message which PROVOKES GREAT OPPOSITION**
   The **agents** of the opposition – **people**
   - religious authorities (13:45, 14:2)
   - God-fearing women (13:50)
   - civic leaders (13:50)
   The **nature** of the opposition – **progressive**
   - jealousy (13:45)
   - abusive talk (13:45; 14:2)
   - incitement to violence (13:50, 14:5)
   What about us? (2 Timothy 3:10–13; John 15:20–21)

3. **A message which CREATES GREAT DIVISION**
   A **community split** (14:4; Matthew 10:34–36) because of
   - human choice (13:39–41, 46; 14:2)
   - divine appointment (13:48)
   Do we keep **both aspects in tension?**

WARNING! **missed opportunities** for
   - salvation (13:38)
   - proclamation (13:47)

6. Miracle, misunderstanding and message

(Acts 14:8–20)

A miracle without a message will always be misunderstood.

1. **The miracle** (verses 8–10)

   Sign and word are **inseparable:**

   - before (3:1–26)

   - after (14:3)

   - during (14:9–10)

   Faith in Jesus who is proclaimed in the word

2. **The misunderstanding** (verses 11–13)

   The **wrong conclusion** caused by

   - culture and religion

   - language

   Paul and Barnabas also misunderstand

3. **The message** (verses 14–18)

   An attempt to **correct the misunderstanding**

   - '**we** *are only men,* **human** *like you*'

   - **God** is the **Creator** and **sustainer**

   So, **accept the good news** and **turn from idols to God**

After the miracle (verses 19–20)

   - the **fickle crowd** – few believe (see 16:1)

   - the **faithful witness** – suffering for Christ (Gal. 6:17)

7. Mission accomplished
(Acts 14:21–28)

Paul and Barnabas retrace their steps and return home, **their mission accomplished.** **Four stages** in church–planting

1. **Missionaries must be sent**
   The **commission of Jesus** (Matthew 28:18–20)
   • to **all Christians** (2 Corinthians 2:14 – 3:3)
   • to **'apostles',** sent by the church (see 13:1–3)
   This is **essential** – Romans 10:12–15

2. **The gospel must be preached**
   The **saving facts** about Jesus are proclaimed so that
   • some **respond and believe,** and are
   • brought into a **relationship with other believers**
   and **a church is born**

3. **Believers must be discipled**
   New Christians must be
   • **'strengthened'** and
   • **'encouraged** *to remain true to the faith'*
   because they will **face many hardships**   (verse 22)

4. **Churches must be led**
   'Elders' are appointed (see Titus 1:5)
   • **local**
   • **plural**
   • **new Christians!**
   The **missionaries' confidence** – see verse 23

Reporting back (verses 26–28)
   • **used by God**
   • **an open door**

12

The Prince of Egypt
(Exodus 1-19)

Genesis – the first book of the Bible – ends with hope. God's chosen people, the descendants of Abraham, are providentially preserved from famine in Canaan by Joseph who has become Prime Minister in Egypt. In Egypt they prosper and await the day when they will return to the Promised Land, carrying the embalmed body of Joseph with them.

Exodus – the second book of the Bible – begins with despair. The Israelites, by now a vast community, are enslaved in Egypt by a new Pharaoh 'who did not know about Joseph'. Their prospects look grim but it is through their adversity that the Lord will uproot them from Egypt and set them on pilgrimage – back to Canaan.

The Exodus is the key event in Israel's history and the key figure who is instrumental in leading the people of Israel during this crucial period is Moses. Prepared by prosperity, living as 'the son of Pharaoh's daughter' for the first forty years of his life, and also by adversity, living in obscurity as a shepherd for the next forty years of his life, he is finally equipped for the final forty years of his life as he leads the people of Israel through their wilderness wanderings to the edge of the Promised Land.

These events are of great significance in salvation-history – not only for Jews, who revere Moses as their greatest leader, but also for Christians, who worship Jesus as their Lord. Jesus spoke of his own 'exodus' (Luke 9:31) to Moses (and Elijah) and the greater salvation that he would provide.

The characteristics and failings of the people of Israel bear sad and striking parallels with those of the people of God in every generation and under the New Covenant. And those who have the responsibility of leadership can also find parallels in the example of Moses – things to emulate and also avoid. The title 'The Prince of Egypt' was borrowed and prompted by the film of that name,

and partly chosen for its topicality. The series concluded with the Israelites approaching Mount Sinai before the giving of the Law, which the New Testament contrasts with 'coming to Mount Zion' under the New Covenant (Hebrews 12:28–29).

A useful commentary is the Mentor Commentary on *Exodus* by John L. Mackay. The author interacts with other scholars in either text or footnotes. In addition to exploring the meaning of the text he examines the chronology, authorship, composition and structure of Exodus. In addition, at the end of each section he provides a reflective comment.

The Tyndale Old Testament Commentary by Alan Cole (Tyndale Press, 1973) is a helpful (if rather brief) commentary on the text. More detailed is the Word Biblical Commentary by John I. Durham (Word, 1987) which also includes the author's own translation of the text.

For preachers, Charles R. Swindoll's *Moses – a Man of Selfless Dedication* (Word, 1999) has many challenging insights and applications, even though from an American context. More dated, and not appealing to all, is A. W. Pink's *Gleanings in Exodus* (Moody Press, 1981). Also dated, and from a Christian Brethren typological approach is John Ritchie *From Egypt to Canaan* (John Ritchie Ltd, 1999).

1. Hard times
(Exodus 1)

Seeing the events from **the right perspective**

1. The God of history
God **uses circumstances to fulfil his plan** (Genesis 50:19–20)
- the **prosperity** of the Israelites (verses 6–7)
- the **hostility** of a new king (verses 8–10)
    — slavery (verses 11–14)
    — infanticide (verses 15–21)
    — murder (verse 22)

The **Christian's assurance** – Romans 8:28–39

2. The God of covenant
God **remembers his promises** (2:23–25)
- the **call of Abram** (Genesis 12:1–3)
- the **future foretold** (Genesis 15:12–16)
- **reassurance** to Jacob (Genesis 46:1–4)
- **future hope,** despite death (Gen.49:29–50:14; 50:24–25)

The **promise that will be kept** – 2 Peter 3:3–13

3. The God of salvation
God **sends a deliverer** (3:7–10)
- the **birth of a baby** (2:1–2)
- Moses – **'no ordinary child'** (Hebrews 11:23)

God **sends his Son** to **turn slaves into sons** – Galatians 4:4–7

2. 'No ordinary child'
(Exodus 2)

What his parents *'saw by faith'* – Hebrews 11:23

1.   **God's protection**
      God **used people** and **means**:
      • **Moses' mother** for three months
          —   in the home
          —   in the river
      • **Pharaoh's daughter** for forty years
          —   in the home
          —   in the palace
The **assurance of God's people** – Psalm 139; Luke 12:4–7

2.   **God's preparation**
      Two **radically different places**
      • in the **home**
          —   his **Hebrew heritage**
          —   his **mother's role**
      • in the **palace**
          —   his **Egyptian education** (Acts 7:22)
          —   **Pharaoh's plan**
The   **right   choice**   and   **motive**   (Hebrews   11:24–26);
but the **wrong** means and **moment**

3.   **God's promise**
      God's plan (Genesis 15:13–14) is **still in place**
      • Moses' **protection** still continues (verse 15)
      • Moses' **preparation** still continues (2:21 – 3:1)
      —   the **desert** (Matthew 4:1–11)–   **character development**
      —   the **shepherd** (1 Peter 5:2–4) – **skill training**
God's time at last (verses 23–25) – for **Moses** and **the Israelites**

3. The call of Moses
(Exodus 3:1 – 4:17)

A **momentous meeting** – for Moses, and the world!

1. The burning bush (3:1–10)
GOD takes the initiative (verses 1–3)
- he **speaks** (verses 4–6)
- he **reveals himself** (verses 7–9)
  - — his **holiness** (Deuteronomy 4:24; Heb.12:28–29)
  - — his **love** (34:5–7; Romans 5:6–8)

God **sends a 'saviour'** (verse 10; John 3:16–17)

2. The reluctant rescuer (3:11 – 4:13)
MOSES raises objections
- **inadequacy** (3:11–12) – *'Who am I?'*
  - — God's **presence**
  - — God's **promise**
- **authority** (3:12–21) – *'Who are you?'*
  - — God's **name** – I AM
  - — **past** and **future**
- **credibility** (4:1–9) – *'What if they don't believe me?'*
  - — the sign of the **staff** that becomes a **snake**
  - — the sign of the **hand** that becomes **diseased**
  - — the sign of the **water** that becomes **blood**
- **inability** (4:10–12) – *'I am slow of speech'*
  - — God's **questions**
  - — God's **command** and **promise**

Moses **doesn't want to go** (verse 13)

The outcome (verses 14–17)
- God's **anger** with Moses
- God's **persistence** with Moses

4. True worship
(Exodus 4:18 – 6:27)

1. Worship the one true God

- no special cases (4:24–26; cf. Genesis 17:12–14)

- the God who redeems (6:6–8; cf. 12:43–48)

- the same Gospel in the Old Testament and the New Testament (4:21–23)
  — your son for my Son (John 3:16)

2. Worship that is shallow

- self–centred worship (4:29–31)

- the heart is revealed (5:19 – 6:1; Isaiah 29:13)

- words are cheap (Ecclesiastes 5:4–5)

3. Worship that is a response

- free...to worship God (4:23; 5:1)

- preparations for worship (6:13–27; cf. 1 Chronicles 23:13–14)

Why and how do you worship God?

5. The hardening of the spiritual arteries
(Exodus 7–10)

The ten plagues – **God's answer to Pharaoh's question** (5:2)

Three symptoms of *'the hardening of the heart'* to the word of the Lord

1.   **Absolute rejection**

A **refusal**

- to **listen** (7:13, 22; 8:15, 19, etc.)

- to **obey** (9:7; 10:20, etc.)

The **natural rebellion** of the human heart (Genesis 3; Psalm 2)

2.   **Apparent capitulation**

Changes of mind prompted by

- the **sending** of adversity (8:8, 28; 9:27, 10:16, etc.)

- the **removal** of adversity (8:12–15; 9:33–35; 10:18–20)

Repentance or **remorse?** (2 Corinthians 7:10; Hebrews 12:15–17)

3.   **Attempted negotiation**

Suggested **compromises**

- *'sacrifice...here in the land...not very far'* (8:25–28)

- *'let only the men go'* (10:8–11)

- *'only leave your flocks and herds behind'* (10:24–26)

Complete obedience essential (Matthew 6:24; Romans 12:1–2)

FINAL WARNING! (Psalm 95:7–11; Hebrews 3:7–11)

6. Freedom at midnight
(Exodus 11:1 – 13:16)

The Passover – *'What does this ceremony mean?'* (12:26–27)

1. Propitiation

The **death of the firstborn son:**

- the **justice** of God the **Judge** – **death** (12:29)

- the **mercy** of God the **Saviour** – **life** (12:21–23)

The **death of God's Son** (John 1:29; 1 John 4:10)

2. Preservation

The **blood of the lamb**

- not only **shed** (Hebrews 9:22)

- but also ***'sprinkled'*** (Hebrews 11:28)

'Faith in his blood' (Romans 3:21–26)

3. Preparation

'The Feast of Unleavened Bread' (12:14–20; 13:3–10)

- starting a new life

- getting rid of the old life

'Keeping the Festival' (1 Corinthians 5:6–8; Luke 22:7–20)

7. Between the desert and deep Red Sea
(Exodus 13:17 – 14:31)

Three ways in which the Lord acts to save his people

1. **The route by which he took them (13:17–22)**
    The Lord **led his people** (verses 20–22)

    • to the land he promised (verse 19; Genesis 50:24–26; Joshua 24:32) **but**

      • not by the shortest route (verses 17–18)
    The Lord **still leads his people** (John 16:13; Acts 13:1–3)

2. **The place to which he led them (14:1–14)**
    To an *'impossible'* situation in order to *'gain glory'* for himself (verses 4, 17, 31)

      • in **judgement** – on those who **refuse** his word (verses 3–4)
      • in **salvation** – for those who **obey** his word (vv.13–14)
    The Lord **still works in the same way** (2 Corinthians 1:8–10)

3. **The deliverance which he brought them (14:15–31)**
    The miracle **shows the difference** (Hebrews 11:29) between:
      • **saving faith**, which leads to **life** (verses 21–22), and
      • **presumption**, which leads to **death** (verses 23–28)
    The **greatest miracle** (Ephesians 1:19–23) – and **our response to it?** (Romans 6:1–14)

A **final warning** – 1 Corinthians 10:1–13

8. Singing – and grumbling
(Exodus 15)

Contrasting responses to God's guidance – within three days!

1. **SINGING** – when the Lord SAVES his people (vv. 1–21)

   A song of praise to the Lord **the** warrior **who**

   - judges **those who have** opposed **him** (vv. 1–12)

   - leads **those who he has** redeemed (vv. 13–18)

   The song that is sung in heaven **(Revelation 15:1–4)**

2. **GRUMBLING – when the Lord TESTS his people (vv. 22-27)**

   Facing difficulty and disappointment

   - previous **failure** – a *'re–sit'* **(Exodus 14)**

   - present **failure – poor memories**

   - future **failure** – a repeated pattern **(16:1–3, etc.)**

   Yet the Lord graciously answers

The lesson **that the Lord wants to teach his people** – praise in all circumstances **(Psalm 34:1; 1 Thessalonians 5:16–18)**

9. The message of the miracle
(Exodus 16)

Three important matters about the *'bread from heaven'*

1. **It was a gift they did not deserve**

   The Lord's **gracious gift** to the Israelites despite

   - their **bad memories** about the past (verse 3)
   - their **constant grumbling** against him (verses 6–8)

   Experiencing God's grace (Ephesians 2:8–9; Hebrews 4:14–16)

2. **It was a test they did not pass**

   The importance of following the Lord's instructions for

   - daily **dependence** (Matthew 6:11)
   - Sabbath **observance** (Exodus 20:8–11)

   The consequences of disobedience (Exodus 32)

3. **It was a lesson they did not learn**

   Not how the miracle was performed but why.

   - **proof** – *'then you will know ....'* (verse 12)
   - yet **unbelief** – *'Is the Lord among us or not?'* (17:7)

   An **even greater tragedy** (John 6:25–59, 20:30–31)

What about us? (Hebrews 3:7–19)

10. Testing the Lord
(Exodus 17:1–7)

Two *'test–questions'* in a **time of crisis**

1. *'Why did you bring us up out of Egypt to make us die of thirst?'*

Questioning the **purpose** of the Lord (verses 1–4)

- **grumbling** against the Lord

- **quarrelling** with the Lord

- **rebelling** against the Lord

Does God **love me?**

2.   *'Is the Lord among us or not?'*

Questioning the **presence** of the Lord (verses 5–7)

- **receiving** an **answer** from the Lord

- **obeying** the **word** of the Lord

- **enjoying** the **provision** of the Lord

Will God **help me?**

God's answer for the Christian

- greater **love** – the **death** of Jesus

- greater **power** – the **resurrection** of Jesus

- greater **evidence** – less **excuse**

Unbelief – or **faith?**   (Hebrews 3:7–19)

11. Sharing the burden
(Exodus 18:1–27)

The **context** – *'growing pains'* arising out of great blessing (vv. 1–12)

1. **A serious problem (verses 13–18)**

    - for the **leader**

    - for the **people**

2. **A sensible solution (verses 19–26)**

    Choosing capable men

    - **teaching** God's law

    - **delegating** responsibility

    Everybody satisfied

3. **An important principle**

    The **role of the leader**

    - **training** and **equipping** (Ephesians 4:11–16)

    - **delegating** and **prioritising** (Acts 6:1–7)

    The **result:growth** and **maturity**

12. Coming to the mountain
(Exodus 19)

Coming to Mount Sinai (verses 1–2) – to **meet with the Lord**

1.   **Condescension (verses 3–9)**
    The **initiatives** the Lord **takes**
- **choosing** the people of Israel
  - *'my treasured possession'*
  - *'a kingdom of priests'*
  - *'a holy nation'*
- ***'coming down'***
  - to the mountain
  - to Moses

2.   **Consecration (verses 10–15)**
    The **preparations** the Lord **demands**
- the **demands** of holiness (Leviticus 11:44–45; 1 Peter 1:16) – **cleansing** of body and clothing
- the **danger** of holiness (3:1–5; Hebrews 10:31) – **setting limits**

3.   **Communication (verses 14–25)**
    The **words** the Lord **speaks** (20:1ff)
- given **through Moses** (Deuteronomy 5:23–27)
- **total obedience** required (Deuteronomy 5:32–33)

Broken **promises** – broken **laws** (Exodus 32)

Coming to 'MOUNT ZION' (Hebrews 12:18–27)
- a **better covenant** – through **Jesus** (John 1:17)
- a **greater judgement** – for **refusal**

The appropriate response – **acceptable worship** (Hebrews 12:28–29)

13

Believe it or not!
(John's Gospel)

No one disputes the fact that the fourth gospel has a radically different perspective from the other three – hence their common description as 'synoptic' gospels. What is hotly disputed is the purpose for which John wrote his Gospel and numerous theories abound.

However, if we take the gospel itself at face-value, then, rather than seeing it as some esoteric tract with a hidden meaning for Christians, we should instead recognise it as a selective account of the life of Jesus written with an evangelistic purpose in mind. This is made clear by the final verses of the gospel (before what many believe is the added resurrection appearance of chapter 21):

> Jesus did many other miraculous signs in the presence of his disciples, which are not recorded in this book. But these are written that you may believe that Jesus is the Christ, the Son of God, and that by believing you may have life in his name. (John 20:30–31)

The key word in the gospel which reinforces the view that it is evangelistic in purpose is the verb 'believe' and its cognates. With this in mind, we made a modest attempt to preach the gospel evangelistically by selecting key passages which focused on the response of faith. Along with this, we planned 'seeker friendly' services which included interviews with individuals whose story (where possible) paralleled those in focus in the gospel. And, in a radical departure (for us!), recognising that many younger people today get their morality from television programmes like 'Friends', our drama-group wrote a series called 'Breakfast in Balerno' in which a group of young people sharing a flat in Edinburgh addressed some of the issues arising out of the passage and in preparation for the message which followed.

There is a wealth of excellent material on John's Gospel, more than for any other gospel. The two commentaries I found most helpful were Leon Morris in the New International Commentary (Eerdmans, 1995) and, best of all, D. A. Carson (IVP, 1991) .

1. From eternity to here!
(John 1:1–18)

Three themes about **GOD**

1. **ETERNAL**
    'In the beginning....' (verse 1; Genesis 1:1)

    Two kinds of evidence for God's existence
    - **objective** – the universe (verse 3; Romans 1:20)
    - **subjective** – inner *'light'* (verse 4; Genesis 1:26–27)

    Yet still we **cannot fully understand** (Ecclesiastes 3:11)

2. **TEMPORAL**
    'The Word became flesh and made his dwelling among us' (verse 14)

    The Eternal God has **stepped into time**
    - **divine** (verses 1–3)
    - **distinct** (verse 14)

    Jesus – **God's self–portrait** (verse 18)

3. **PERSONAL**
    'Yet to all who received him, who believed in his name' (verse 12)

    Two possible responses
    - **rejection** (verses 10–11)
    - **reception** (verses 12–13)
        — a change of **status**
        — a change of **nature** (John 3:3)

    A **decisive moment**

2. 'PC – A new man?'
(John 1:35–42)

Three life changes:

1. **A New TEACHER   (1:35–39)**

   • jumping ship?   (John 3:25–30)

   • *'What do you want?'*

   • *'Where are you staying?'*

2. **A New INVITATION (1:40–41)**

   • for...a Big Brother

   • to...the Messiah

3. **A New NAME   (1:42)**

   • **'You are**...*Simon, Son of John'* (13:6–10, 18:25–27)

   • **'You will be**...*called Cephas'*   (21:15–19)

3. Pride and prejudice
(John 1:43–51)

An **enthusiast** (Philip) and a **sceptic** (Nathanael)

1. *'Come and see'* – **AN OPEN MIND** (verses 43–46)

    Nathanael's objection – **Nazareth!**

    *   obscure?

    *   no prophecy?

    *   inter–town rivalry? (21:2)

        Philip's answer – **a meeting with Jesus**

2. *'I saw you'* – **AN OPEN LIFE** (verses 47–49)

    Jesus **knows** Nathanael

    *   his character (Genesis 26:26; 27:36)

    *   his experience (Psalm 139)

        Nathanael's **confession** – *'Rabbi...Son of God...King of Israel'*

3. *'You will see'* – **AN OPEN HEAVEN** (verses 50–51)

    The **promise** of Jesus

    *   background – Genesis 28:10–22

    *   fulfilment – Mark 15:21–41

    'Greater things' – enough **evidence for everyone** (20:30–31)

4. 'Born-again christians –
Are there any other kinds?'
(John 3:1–21)

The context – a conversation between Jesus and a religious Jew.
Three facts about being *'born again':*

1.   **It is absolutely essential –**
      'you must be born again' (verses 3, 5 & 7)
      Emphatic words from Jesus (verses 3, 5 & 11) – no one
can
      • *'see the kingdom of God'* (verse 3)

      • *'enter the kingdom of God'* (verse 5)
      A hard lesson for a Pharisee!

2.   **It is humanly conceivable –**
      'how can a man be born when he is old?' (verse 4)

      The **answer of Jesus**
      • not **physical** but **spiritual** (verses 5–6; 1:12–13)

      • not **human** but **divine** (verse 7; Mark 9:17–31)

      • not **understandable** but **observable** (verses 8–9; 1
            John)
      *'How can this **happen**?'* (verse 9)

3.   **It is wonderfully possible –**
      'God so loved the world that he gave...' (verse 16)
      The **gift of God**
      • his one and only **Son** (verses 11–13)

      • his **death** on the cross (verses 14–16; see Numbers
            21:4–9)

      • eternal **life** (Romans 6:23)

Believe him – or **not!** (verses 17–21)

5. Satisfaction guaranteed
(John 4:1–42)

The promise – *'living water'* which completely satisfies (verses 13–14)

1.   **A thirsty man (verses 1–10)**

     'Will you give me a drink?'

     *   the **humanity** of Jesus
     *   the **humility** of Jesus

     Jesus the Jew who offers *'God's gift'* to a Samaritan woman

2.   **A thirsty woman (verses 11–26)**

     'Sir, give me this water'

     *   unfulfilling **relationships**
     *   uninformed **religion**

     Jesus the Messiah who *'explains everything'* **has come**

3.   **A thirsty world (verses 27–42)**

     'Come, see a man...Could this be the Christ?'

     *   the **witness** of the woman
     *   the **'food'** of Jesus
     *   the **'harvest'** of people

     Jesus the Saviour *'of the world'* (3:16–17, 19:28–30)

6. The leap of faith
(John 4:46–53)

1.   Faith is in Jesus   (verse 47)

Desperation drives us to trust (John 11:21)

- ...not in things

- ...not in ourselves

- ...but in a real historical person (John 2:11)

2.   Faith is a leap   (verses 48–49)

- ...but not a leap in the dark   (John 5:31–40)

- it is a reasonable faith   (John 20:30–31)

3.   Faith is a spiral   (verses 50–53)

- faith means obedience   (John 14:15)

- obedience means faith   (John 15:10)

7. It could be you!

(John 5:1–30)

Three important meetings with Jesus

1. **It is you (verses 1–13)**

    'Get up!'

    - many needy people **waiting**
    - one needy man **healed**

    Jesus the **miracle–worker**

2. **It may be you (verses 14–23)**

    'Stop sinning!'

    - something **worse** than sickness
    - something **better** than healing

    Jesus the **Saviour**

3. **It will be you (verses 24–30)**

    'Come out!'

    - **no condemnation** – life
    - **condemnation** – death

    Jesus the **Judge**

8. People who live in glass houses...
(John 7:53 – 8:11)

Three important questions:

1. **To stone or – or not to stone?** (verses 2–6a)

   A *'trick question'* for Jesus from his religious opponents

   * **'Yes'** – problems with **the Romans**
   * **'No'** – problems with **the Jews**

   A personal question for each of us

2. **To speak – or not to speak?** (verse 6b–9)

   The **response of Jesus**

   * **bending and writing** – mercy
   * **straightening up and speaking** – judgement

   Everyone must leave for no one is *'without sin'*

3. **To sin – or not to sin?** (verses 10–11)

   The **judgement of Jesus**

   * a change of **status** – no condemnation
   * a change of **lifestyle** – repentance (Luke 3:7–14; Acts 2:38)

   Salvation – or **condemnation?** (John 3:16–18)

9. Seeing is believing
(John 9:1–41)

1. **Suffering is blinding** (verses 1–12)

    •   the **problem**

    •   the **solution**

          — a change in **thinking**

          — a change in **perspective**

          — a change in **healing**

2. **Religion is blinding**   (verses 13–34)

    •   religion as your view of life

    •   when worlds collide!

    •   good and bad arguing

3. **Seeing is believing** (verses 1–41)

    •   admit that you are blind from birth

    •   ask Jesus to open your eyes

    •   grow to understanding who Jesus is

    •   face the consequences!

10. Where there's death, there's hope
(John 11:1–44)

A crisis in the family

1. **Hopeful**
   'Lord, the one you love is sick' (verse 3)
   - A **'telegram'** sent to Jesus in the assurance that
     — he is **able** to help
     — he is **willing** to help
   - A **hopeful reply** – *'this sickness will not end in death'*

2. **Hopeless**
   'Lazarus is dead' (verse 14)
   - **Confusion** and **shock**
     — Jesus **delays** (verse 6)
     — Jesus is **glad** (verse 15)
     — Jesus **arrives** – *if you had been here...' (*vv. 21&32)
   - Is **death the end?**

3. **Hope–filled**
   'I am the resurrection and the life' (verse 25)
   - **Jesus intervenes**
     — the **compassion** of Jesus –*Jesus wept'* (v. 35)
     — the **authority** of Jesus – *'Lazarus, come out!'* (v.43)
   - **The crucial question** – 'Do you believe?' (verse 26, 20:30–31**)**

God's Plan –
*'one man **must die** ....'* (verses 49–53)
   - and **rise again** (Luke 24:5–6)
   - and **return** (1 Thessalonians 4:13–18)

11. Head over heels
(John 12:1–11)

Being a Christian means...

1. **Putting 'Being' before 'Doing' (verses 1–3)**

    • Mary was 'head over heels' – extravagant love!
    • Going with the tide
    • Being a Christian, not 'doing' one!

2. **Being critical, not cynical (verses 4–8)**
    •   Judas the Brit – cynical to the core!
          — evaluating, not destroying
          — honest, not bringing everyone else down
          — not ruled by past experiences

    going against the tide

    barn–raising or clay–pigeon shooting?

3. **Being head over heels! (verses 1–3)**

    • bowing your **head** in submission (19:30; Isaiah 58:5)

    • falling at his **feet** in worship(Revelation 1:17–18)

12. Pilate errors
(John 18:28 – 19:16)

Three issues in the trial before Pilate

1. **The identity of Jesus (18:28–37a)**
   'Are you the King of the Jews?' (18:33)

   • a different **kind of king**

   • a different **kind of kingdom**

   Understanding **who Jesus is**

2. **The authority of Jesus (18:37b – 19:11)**
   'Don't you realise I have the power....' (19:10)

   • the **words** of Jesus – Pilate in the dock! (18:37)

   • the **silence** of Jesus – Jesus in control (18:8–11)

   Obeying **what Jesus says**

3. **The destiny of Jesus (19:12–16)**
   'Shall I crucify your king?' (19:15)

   • **Pilate's** decision **and**

   • **God's** plan (Acts 4:24–28)

   Repenting of **what we have done** (Acts 2:36–40)

13. Surprised by joy
(John 20:1–18)

A totally unexpected event

1.   **The missing man (verses 1–9)**
     Evidence **at the tomb** – Jesus **absent**

   - the stone removed (verse 1)
   - the grave clothes present (verses 6–7)
   - the body gone (verse 8)

'He is not here; he has risen!' (1 Corinthians 15:14–20)

2.   **The weeping woman (verses 10–16)**
     Evidence **from experience** – Jesus **present**

   - repeated question (verses 13 & 15a)
   - limited understanding (verse 15b)
   - personal address (verse 16)

'I have seen the Lord!' (verse 18)

3.   **The living Lord (verses 17–18)**
     Evidence **for the future** – Jesus **ascended**

   - *'my brothers'* (Hebrews 2:9–11)
   - *'my Father and your Father, my God and your God'* (Romans 8:15–16)

'What I received I passed on to you....' (1 Corinthians 15:1–8)

14. Seeing is not believing
(John 20:24–31)

How do we move from then to now?

1.   **Thomas – belief in physical reality (verses 24–25)**

- *'Doubting Thomas'*   (John 11:16; 14:5)

- *'Unless I see..and touch..'*

- Gracious Jesus

2.   **Jesus – reality changes (verses 26–28)**

- a magic act?

- Jesus is more real   (Luke 24:37–43)

- believe in what is real

3.   **Us – belief in Jesus   (verses 29–31)**

- the one and the many

- seeing is **not** believing

  — the evidence of *'this book'*

  — belief in Jesus as the Christ, the Son of God

14

The Coming King
(The early life of David)

One of the most difficult tensions to live with is between the promises of God and their fulfilment. This is true in its broadest context as the people of God live between the two comings of Christ – between his advent and his return. Yet it is also true on a personal and individual level.

However, this 'gestation-period' is not wasted time. In God's economy it is used by him to shape the person and prepare him or her for whatever future ministry may lie ahead.

Nowhere is this more clearly seen than in the early life of David. He is only a teenager when he is anointed by a prophet to be the future King of Israel to replace the rejected Saul. Yet it is many years before David finally inherits the kingdom. In this period he is prepared and shaped by God to become Israel's greatest king. In it he learns invaluable lessons – patience, trust in God, leadership skills and many more. Much of what David learned we too can learn from – not least from many of the Psalms he wrote during this period, songs of praise and prayers for help to the Lord his God.

The Tyndale Old Testament Commentary on 1 & 2 Samuel by Joyce Baldwin (IVP 1988) is a useful resource on the text. The Welwyn Commentary Series by Gordon Keddie on 1 Samuel (*Dawn of a Kingdom*, Evangelical Press, 1988) and 2 Samuel (*Triumph of the King*, Evangelical Press, 1990) have an additional material for the preacher.

Dale Ralph Davis has written two brilliant guides for expositors and preachers on 1 Samuel – *Looking on the Heart* (Baker Books, 1994) and 2 Samuel *Out of Every Adversity* (Christian Focus, 1999).

John Calvin's Sermons on 2 Samuel (chapters 1–13) has been translated by Douglas Kelly and issued by Banner of Truth (1992). Finally, there is a fascinating book on leadership based on Saul, David and Absalom by Gene Edwards – *A Tale of Three Kings* Tyndale House, 1980, 1992).

We concluded the series with a focus on **the** Coming King – the Lord Jesus Christ with the journey of the Magi from Matthew 2 and his future return from Revelation 22.

1. Rejected by the Lord
(1 Samuel 15)

Four steps on the downward path away from God:

1. **AN INCOMPLETE OBEDIENCE** (verses 1–11)
   Saul **knew what he should do**
   - the word of the Lord (verses 1–3)
   - the history of Israel (Joshua 6–8)

   But he **failed to obey the Lord fully** (verse 9)

2. **AN INSENSITIVE CONSCIENCE** (verses 12–23)
   Saul **failed to recognise what he had done**
   - the end of a process (see 13:1–15)
   - making excuses and blaming others (Genesis 3:11–13)

   The **Lord's verdict** – *'divination'* and *'idolatry'*

3. **AN INSINCERE REPENTANCE** (verses 24–33)
   Saul admits his sin but **his words show that he**
   - fears the threats of men more than he fears the word of the Lord (Luke 12:4–5)
   - loves the praise of men more than the praise of God (John 12:42–43)

   In contrast, **Samuel leads by example** (verses 32–33)

4. **AN IRREVOCABLE CONSEQUENCE** (verses 34–35)
   A **seeming contradiction**
   - the Lord **'repents'** (verses 10 & 35; Genesis 6:6) – a chosen king (10:1) **rejected** (verses 26–28a)
   - the Lord **'does not repent'** (verse 29; Numbers 23:19) – a chosen king **selected** (verse 28b; 13:14, 16:1–13)

A **stark warning** – Saul **can no longer hear the word of the Lord** (Psalm 95:7; Hebrews 4:7)

2. Hail to the Lord's anointed!'
(1 Samuel 16)

The Lord is **still in control**

1. **A REASSURING WORD** (verses 1–4)

    The Lord has **already chosen a new king** (15:28)

    - a time for **mourning** – now over
    - a time for **action** – time to move
    - a time for **prudence** – take care!

    The King **installed** (Psalm 2)

2. **A SURPRISING CHOICE** (verses 4–12)

    The Lord **sees things differently**

    - not **outward** – *'appearance'* or *'height'* (9:1–2)
    - but **inward** – *'the heart'* (13:14)

    The King **rejected** (Isaiah 52:13 – 53:4; 1 Peter 2:7–8)

3. **AN UNFOLDING PLAN** (verses 13–23)

    The Lord **gives his Spirit for future service**

    - **the shepherd** with his flock
        - knowing the Lord (Psalm 23)
        - fighting the foe (17:34–37)
        - governing the people (Psalm 78:70–72)
    - **the armour–bearer/ musician** at court
        - increasing **prominence**
        - increasing **conflict**

    The King **anointed** (Luke 3:21–22)

3. Not by sword or spear
(1 Samuel 17)

The lesson the story is meant to teach – *'the battle is the Lord's'*

1. THE LORD'S NAME DISHONOURED

The **real issues** (verse 26)

- the living God **defied**
- the people of God **disgraced**

The **right priorities** – Matthew 6:9–10

2. THE LORD'S ANOINTED DISCLOSED

The **Lord has a plan** (and **a person**) in place

- **providence** (verses 17–24)
- **preparation** (verses 34–37)
  — practical experience
  — theological training

David's confidence – verse 37

3. THE LORD'S VICTORY DISPLAYED

The kind of person **God chooses – and uses** (16:7)

- **word** (verses 45–47)
- **action** (verses 48–51)
- The **greatest victory** – 1 Corinthians 1:18–31; Colossians 2:13–15

4. The green-eyed monster
(1 Samuel 18 & 19)

Success always brings **choices**

1. Success can bring jealousy (18:9)

The **downward spiral** of Saul's green–eyed monster

- Step 1 – comparison   (18:8)

- Step 2 – jealousy (18:9)

- Step 3 – blind hatred   (19:1)

But **David** doesn't let it go to his head!

2. Success may bring covenant love   (18:3)

- Jonathan honours his rival above himself (18:4)

- Michal protects David at her own risk   (19:17)

3. The King always brings division (19:4, 17)

- Jesus must become greater   (John 3:30)

- Jesus came to divide families (Luke 12:51–53)

5. On the run
(1 Samuel 20–22)

The context :David's life again threatened by Saul (19:9–24)

1.   **Promise in a covenant (Chapter 20)**

Covenant promises (18:3–4) **renewed**

• **selfless** love

• **sacrificial** love

A **better covenant** (Hebrews 10:19–23), and a **greater love** (Romans 5:5–11)

2.   **Panic in a crisis (Chapter 21)**

Running *'by sight'* (not *'walking by faith'*)

• endangering **the lives of others** (verses 1–9, 22:6–22)

• endangering **your own life** (verses 10–15)

Yet **God fulfils his word** (2:27–38, 3:11–18; Acts 2:22–24)

3.   **Preparation in a cave (Chapter 22)**

David **returns to his own land and people**

• **practical** preparation

— his parents (verses 3–4; Ruth 4:18–22)

— his army (verses 1–2; 2 Samuel 23:8–39)

• **spiritual** preparation

— **Psalms 34 & 56** (21:10–15)

— **Psalm 52** (verses 20–22)

— **Psalms 57 & 142** (verses 1–2)

The **next step** (verse 5) – **by faith**

6. The parting of the ways
(1 Samuel 23–24 & 26)

The Lord is **with David** – and **not Saul.**   David is

1. **Directed by the Lord**

    David **seeks, receives and follows the Lord's guidance**

    * when to move (22:5) and when to attack (23:1–6)
    * what will happen and what to do (23:9–12)
    Contrast Saul – **frustrated** and **misled** (23:5, 21)

2. **Protected by the Lord**

    David is **absolutely secure** (23:14) **despite**

    * cowardice (23:12) and betrayal (23:19–20, 26:1)
    * intensive efforts (23–24, 26) and superior forces (24: 2, 26:2)
    Contrast Saul – completely **vulnerable** (24:3, 26:7)

3. **Tested by the Lord**

    David will not disobey the Lord (24:6, 26:9–11) **despite**

    * repeated opportunities (24 & 26)
    * encouragement from others (24:4, 26:8)
    Contrast Saul – **impatience** (13:1–15) and **disobedience** (15: 1–23)

Different destinations – 1 Samuel 31 & 2 Samuel 5 (Matthew 7:13–14)

7. A rose between two thorns
(1 Samuel 25)

How do we **break out of the vicious cycle of repaying evil for evil?**

1. A foolish thorn   (verses 2–3, 25)

- Nabal the rich fool   (verses 2–3, 10–11, 36)

- a fool to reject the Lord's command   (Luke12:16–31)

2. A vengeful fool   (verses 22, 26)

- David the champion of justice?   (verse 21)

- 'do not repay anyone evil for evil'   (Romans 12:17–21)

- past success does not prevent future failure (John 18:10–18)

3. A peacemaking rose   (verses 23–35)

- Abigail to peacemaker (James 3:18)

- in the reconciliation business (2 Cor. 5:18–21)

8. Caught in the web
(1Samuel 27:1 – 28:2; 29:1 – 30:8)

1. **David's web of deceit**   **(1 Samuel 27 & 29)**

   • stopped trusting in the Lord's promises (16; 24:20; 27:1)

   • 'talking to yourself' (27:1)

   • a godless plan (compare 30:6–8)

2. **Caught in the web**   **(1 Samuel 28:1–2; 29)**

   • 'reaping what you sow' (Galatians 6:7–9)

   • David the politician – lying with the truth

   • caught on the horns of a dilemma (Matthew 6:24)

3. **God's web of grace and mercy**   **(1 Samuel 29:1 – 30:8)**

   • David got what he did not deserve (29:10)

   • David did not get what he did deserve (27:8 – compare 30:2)

   • caught in God's web! (30:6–8)

9. Into the night
(1 Samuel 28:3–25)

Saul's crisis (28:3–25) – framed by (and contrasted with) **that of David** (27:1 – 28:2 & 29:1–11)

1. **A distressing situation**
    The **source of Saul's 'terror'**
    * the **shouts** of the Philistines (verses 4–5)
    * the **silence** of the Lord (verse 6; see verse 15b)
    Compare Luke 23:8–9

2. **A desperate measure (verses 7–14)**
    God's law (Leviticus 19:31, 20:6; Deut. 18:9–13)
    * **enforced** by Saul at the **beginning** of his reign (verse 3)
    * **broken** by Saul at the **end** of his reign (verses 7–11)
    'Samuel' is **'brought up'** (verses 12–14)

3. **A devastating message**
    The prophet declares the **unchanging word of the Lord**
    * **what** will happen (verses 17 & 19)
      — dispossession
      — defeat
      — death
    * **why** it will happen (verses 16 & 18; 15:22–23)
      — disobedience

4. **A dreadful tragedy**
    The word of the Lord fulfilled
    * the last **meal** (verses 15–20; compare John 13:18–30)
    * the last **battle** (31:1–13)

Saul's epitaph – and **hope for the future** :1 Chr. 10:13–14

God's final Word (Mark 15:33–39) and **warning** (Hebrews 10:26–31)

10. Good or bad news?
(2 Samuel 1)

News from the battle (verses 1–10; 1 Samuel 31; 1 Chronicles 10:1–14)
David's **godly response**

1. **The attitude he adopted (verses 11–12)**

   A **genuine grief** for Saul (and Israel)

   • motivated by spiritual not selfish concern

   • settled long ago (1 Samuel 24:9–15, 26:23–24)

   The **challenge for the Christian** – Matthew 5:23–26, 43–48

2. **The action he took (verses 13–16)**

   A **just judgement** based on the Amalekite's testimony

   • killing the Lord's anointed? or

   • deceit and self–interest

   Contrast David with **Saul** (1 Samuel 28:18–19)

3. **The anguish he expressed (verses 17–27)**

   A **lasting lament** for future generations

   • **Saul** – only what is praiseworthy

   • **Jonathan** – love and loyalty

   The **real tragedy** – the Lord's name dishonoured

Good news to come:

   • a new king – **David** (2 Samuel 5:1–5)

   • the king – **Jesus** (Matthew 2:2)

The **never–ending kingdom** (Isaiah 9:2–7)

11. The route to the throne
(2 Samuel 2:1 – 3:5)

Saul is dead (1:1–10), but it will be **over seven years before David is crowned as king over all Israel!** (5:1–5).
In the interim, he must **continue to follow the Lord's directions**

1.   **Unhurried preparations (2:1–7)**

A **difficult situation** with an **obvious solution**

- yet David does not rush (Proverbs 19:2),

- but seeks the Lord's will (Proverbs 3:5–6),

- then obeys it

A **public anointing** – but **only by some**

2.   **Unhelpful distractions (2:8 – 3:1)**

A **rival kingdom**

- an ambitious general – Abner (but see 3:17–18)

- a puppet king – Ish-Bosheth

- a foolish young man and his vengeful brother – Asahel and Joab (3:22–39)

The **real losers** – the Israelites;   the **real winners** – the Philistines

3.   **Unhappy relations (3:2–5)**

David's six wives and children **– disobeying God's plan**

- for everyone – Genesis 2:18–24

- for the king – Deuteronomy 17:17

Inevitable consequences – Galatians 6:7–8

The **first and second coronation of the King** (1 Cor.15:20–28)

12. Three men and a murder
(2 Samuel 3:6 – 39)

The **breakdown of human relationships** – cause and effect (James 4:1–3)

1. **Abner – motivated by ambition (verses 6–21)**
   The **decisions Abner took**
   - promoting Ish–Bosheth (2:8– 3:1)
   - challenging for power (3:6–7)
   - changing sides (3:8–21)

   Casualties along the way

2. **Joab – motivated by revenge (verses 22–28)**
   A **totally unjustified crime**
   - a reluctant action in battle (2:18–23)
   - a broken promise of peace (2:26–28)
   - a crime in a *'city of refuge'* (Num.35:9–28; Joshua 20)

   How to **avoid *'giving the devil a foothold'*** (Ephesians 4:22–27)

3. **David – motivated by justice (verses 28–39)**
   What David **said:**
   - about Joab (verses 28–31)
   - about Abner (verses 33–34, 38)

   What David **did:**
   - public mourning (verses 31–34)
   - private grief (verse 35)

Popularity but **limited power** (verse 36–39; 1 Kings 2:5–6; 34)
THE KING and his justice – Isaiah 11:1–10

13. A model king!
(2 Samuel 5:1–12)

1. David the Shepherd-King (verses 1–2)

- recognised as King at last!
  (Deuteronomy 17:15; 2 Samuel 3:9–10)

- David the Shepherd–King
  (Numbers 27:15–18; Psalm 78:70–72)

- Jesus **the** Shepherd–King!
  (Psalm 23:Matthew 2:6; John 10:11)

2. David the King over all Israel   (verses 3 & 12)

- 'established by God'   (1 Samuel 16:13)

- 'for the sake of his people Israel'

- David **not** the King (1 Chronicles 22:8–10; Psalm 16:8–11, 110:1)

- Jesus **the** King! (Matthew 22:41–46; Acts 2:25–35)

3. David the Priest-king   (verses 6–11)

- David captures Jerusalem (Judges 1:8, 21:1; 1 Samuel 17:54)

- King Zedek of Jerusalem? (Genesis 14:18; Joshua 10:1)

- Jesus **the** Priest–King!
  (2 Samuel 8:18; Psalm 110:4; Hebrews 7)

14. Seeking the King
(Matthew 2:1–18)

Opposing reasons for wanting to find *'the one born king of the Jews'*

1. **Seeking the King in order to worship him**
   'Magi from the east'
   - alerted by **a sign** (Numbers 24:17?)
     — its leading – to Israel
     — its limitation – to the palace in Jerusalem
   - redirected by **Scripture** (Micah 5:2)
     — to Bethlehem
     — to the house

   Submission – *'bow down and worship'*   (Psalm 72:10–11)

2. **Seeking the King in order to destroy him**
   King Herod
   - **disturbed**
     — his ignorance
     — his enlightenment
   - **devious**
     — pretended worship
     — intended murder

   Opposition – always ends in **frustration**

A neutral position about the King?
'The chief priests and teachers of the law'
- about the **baby** and his **birth**

but not
- about the **man** and his **death**   (Matthew 27:41–43)

The King lives! – experiencing his **wrath** or his **mercy** (Psalm 2)

15. The Lord is coming!
(Revelation 22)

The **promise of Jesus**:
'I am coming soon' (verses 7, 12 & 20)

1. The final chapter
'He is coming soon' – the **last words of 'revelation'**
- trustworthy and true (verse 6)
- final and unalterable (verses 18–19)

From the **faithful and reliable witness** (verses 13 & 16)

2. The final state
'He is coming soon' – **no time to change**
- wrong or right (verse 11)
- exclusion or inclusion (verses 14b–15)

The **only hope for change now** – verse 14a

3. The final invitation (verse 17)
'He is coming soon' – a **free gift** (Isaiah 55:1–2; John 4:10–14)
- offered **by**
  - *'the Spirit'* and
  - *'the bride'*
- offered **to**
  - *'whoever is thirsty'*
  - *'whoever wishes'*

No time for delay (2 Peter 3:8–10)

4. The final prayer (verses 20–21)
'He is coming soon' – **so we pray**
- *'Come Lord Jesus'* – **future hope** (Romans 8:18–25)
- *'the grace of the Lord Jesus ......'* – **present need**

AMEN!

A SAMPLE SERMON

Ephesus – First Love Forsaken
(Revelation 2:1–7)

To prove that I have at least acculturated a little to my present mission field, I will **begin with a quote** by Scotland's greatest poet. And, to show that I still retain some independence of thought, I will then **disagree with it!**

'O wad some Pow'r the giftie gie us
to see oursels as others see us!'

Robbie Burns was **right in his diagnosis** – we can so easily deceive ourselves. He was **wrong in his solution** because most of us are consummate actors – or, to use the Greek work, *'hypocrites'* – so that we can fool others. Even more alarming, the act can become our reality so that we end up fooling ourselves for, as the prophet Jeremiah said, 'The heart is deceitful above all things and beyond cure. Who can understand it?'(Jeremiah 17:9)

What we need most of all is to **see ourselves as God sees us**. That is why **God has given us his Word and his Spirit** to take that Word and **reveal the true state of things as they really are**. That is true of all of the Bible and it is **especially true of the last book of the Bible**.

Its name is derived from the first word of the book in the original Greek. It is *apokalupsis*, from which name we also have an anglicised word – **Apocalypse**. To most people, an apocalypse is, to quote the dictionary, *'an event of great importance, accompanied by violence'*. But that is not the **primary** meaning. The Greek word is made up of two parts and literally means *'to uncover, to unveil, to reveal what is hidden'*.

So, when a member of the Royal Family opens a new hospital and pulls back the curtain to reveal the plaque which commemorates the event – that is an apocalypse. When I say at the end of a wedding, *'I now pronounce you man and wife'* and *'You may now kiss the bride'* then her veil is lifted to reveal her face – that is an apocalypse!

So **what is it that is revealed** in this apocalypse, the Book of Revelation? Most Christians would answer – *'The future'* – and they would be right. But only in part. Yes, the first verse tells us that God showed his servant, John, *'what must soon take place'*. Yes, he *'is coming with the clouds'* and he will be revealed to all for *'every eye will see him'* (1:8). Yes, certain events **will take place** before that great and final day of the Lord.

But **that is not all**. Running parallel with that future dimension, and indeed preceding it, is a **present revelation**, of **things as they really are**.

That **present reality** is what is **first of all revealed to John** – suffering for Christ on the prison isle of Patmos, the last of the apostles still alive, most of his fellow-disciples already martyrs for Christ.

If you had been a sociologist at the end of the first century, then you would have given the religious sect that followed one Jesus of Nazareth little chance of survival beyond a few years. It appeared to have little prospects. But **appearances were deceptive,** for the one they worshipped is the Lord of glory, the Lord of life and death, the Lord of time and eternity. It is this reality, this revelation that John, the suffering disciple, **needs to see first of all** – that is *'the revelation of Jesus Christ'*.

Who John saw – the risen and exalted Lord Jesus Christ is described within the limits of human language in Chapter 1, verses 9 to 16. No wonder that, at the sight, **John *'falls at his feet as though dead'*.** But the Lord Jesus Christ **graciously touches him and reassures him:**

> When I saw him, I fell at his feet as though dead. Then he placed his right hand on me and said: 'Do not be afraid. I am the First and the Last. I am the Living One; I was dead, and behold I am alive for ever and ever! And I hold the keys of death and Hades. (Rev. 1:17–18)

Yet what has been revealed to John the **suffering apostle** must also be **shared with the suffering church.** So the Lord Jesus says to him:

> 'Write, therefore, what you have seen**, what is now and what will take place later. The mystery of the seven stars that you saw in my right hand and of the seven golden lampstands is this: The seven stars are the angels of the seven churches, and the seven lampstands are the seven churches. (Revelation 1:19–20)

This is not a revelation for the world in general (most of them will sadly never see it until it is too late, and then they will 'mourn' – 1:7) but to the **church in particular,** represented here **by the seven churches.**

Now of course, these letters were addressed, in the first instance, **to real people in real churches in real places** – in the Roman province (not the modern continent) of Asia and we must always begin with that immediate context. But what about **a wider context and application?**

There is a popular view that these seven churches **represent seven successive ages or dispensations of the church through history** from the first century until the return of Christ – or the Rapture, depending on which millennial view you hold (and we won't even attempt to fall out about that!)

Proponents of this view, whoever they are, always tell us that we are **now living in the last or Laodicean age** of the church. So, one of the

best-known modern popularisers of this position, Hal Lindsay, tells us in his book *There's a new world coming* that the sixth age – the Philadelphian – lasted from AD1750–1925 and that the seventh – Laodicean – age began with this century.

Now, **this view has many difficulties**, not least the irrelevance of the previous six ages (other than of historical interest) to us if we are living in the seventh and last age. More importantly, I am **not sure that the church world-wide could be classed as Laodicean**. Perhaps in Britain but not in Latin America or Africa or even Eastern Europe.

I think it is more helpful and accurate to see these seven letters as **a snapshot in time of a cross-section of the state of the church of Jesus Christ in the first century and in all other succeeding centuries and generations.** So, the challenge as we read them today is to ask **which of these churches are we most like?**

Of course, it is unlikely that there will be **an exact match** between a first century and a twenty-first century church but it may well be that the **general thrust** of a particular letter strikes home with a particular accuracy to a present day situation.

When that happens, it is indeed, in the broadest sense of the word, *'revelation'* – the uncovering of that which is hidden from human view, but **absolutely apparent** to the one who, with 'eyes like blazing fire' walks among the seven churches. To each of them he says, *'I know'*.

H. L. Ellison comments:

> The objective word in all the seven letters is 'I know'. All knowledge of ourselves is at the best directed by self–interest, ignorance and prejudice. We see in part and we know in part. Christ's knowledge is complete, objective and constructive. He rebukes so as to restore.

So, with that conviction we turn to the first of the churches that is addressed (in Revelation 2:1–7)– the church in the city of Ephesus.

I begin with **some opening comments on the place to which this letter is addressed – Ephesus**. Stated simply, Ephesus was a **leading city** and a **leading church**:

a. A leading city.

Ephesus was the nearest city to the prison–island of Patmos where John the Apostle received his revelation. However, it may be the first in the list because it was also **the most important city** of the seven. Although Pergamum was officially the capital city of the Roman province of Asia, Ephesus was the largest and most important – or so they claimed with the slogan of *'Ephesus – the first and greatest metropolis of Asia'*.

It was a **major seaport and centre of trade** for the Mediterranean

world and beyond to the East. Its cosmopolitan population of a quarter of a million people lived in a city with a high standard of living and amenities, and enjoyed the privilege of being a free city in the Roman Empire and also an assize town and seat of government.

Moreover, it housed one of the **seven wonders of the ancient world,** the Temple of Artimus (Diana – Latin) and a flourishing religious life. Not that this was at all positive, for religion and license, along with occult and magic were inextricably linked, and the temple courts provided sanctuary for any criminal, no matter what the offence. So Ephesus became a hotbed for criminal gangs and activity, a fact of some concern for the Roman Senate down through the years.

It seemed **unlikely soil for the seed of the gospel** and yet it became the home of:

b. **A leading church.**

The **Apostle Paul visited Ephesus** on his second missionary journey and established a strong and thriving church. He revisited it on his third missionary journey and spent longer in Ephesus than in any other place on his travels – up to three years. Gifted Christians leaders like the wife and husband team of Priscilla and Aquila, and the brilliant Jewish Alexandrian convert, Apollos, were influential members of the church.

The apostle Paul made it his **base for expanded evangelistic enterprises**, and it was later (probably from Rome) that he had written to the church in the New Testament letter we now have – the **Epistle to the Ephesians**. Timothy, Paul's 'son in the faith' became its pastor and, tradition has it, was martyred there in a mob riot.

By around AD66, John the Apostle was resident there (along with Mary, the mother of Jesus) until his exile to Patmos some twenty five years later. And so, it is perhaps also significant that this **first letter is written to John's home church**.

I am sure that he waited with **a mixture of anticipation and apprehension** to hear what the risen Lord **saw in his church** at Ephesus as he walked among the seven golden lampstands:

'To the angel of the church in Ephesus write:
These are the words of him who holds the seven stars in his right hand and walks among the seven golden lampstands.....(v. 1)

The **'stars'** we are told in 1:20 are 'the angels of the seven churches'. But what are the **'angels'**? Time would fail me to tell of all that has been written on this subject: are they guardian angels, or the messengers who carried the letters to the churches, or somehow the embodiment of the spirit of each church.

Perhaps the most popular view is that they are **the pastors or overseers of each congregation**. If so, then the comment of Warren Wiersbe is a pertinent one:

> The Ephesian church had enjoyed some 'stellar' leadership – Paul, Timothy, and the Apostle John himself – but the Lord reminded them that **he** was in control of the ministry, placing the 'stars' where he pleased. How easy it is for a church to become proud and forget that pastors and teachers are God's gifts (Eph. 4:1) who may be taken away at any time. Some churches need to be cautioned to worship the Lord and not their pastor!

So, **what does the Lord have to say to this church (and to us)?** Let me try and summarise the message to Ephesus under **the title 'First Love Forsaken'** and to divide the contents under **three headings**

      1. **Commendation** (verses 2–3 & 6)
      2. **Criticism** (verse 4)
      3. **Correction** (verse 5a)

We will **look at each in turn**:

1. COMMENDATION (verses 2–3, 6)

The Lord **graciously begins**, not as we so often do when we tackle someone who has done wrong, with **criticism**, but with **praise**. Yes, he has strong words of **denunciation** to say to them, but they are **framed with affirmation**. In the first half of verse 2 there is a **general commendation**:

I know your deeds, your hard work and your perseverance.
Then he goes on to give **more specific details**:

> I know that you cannot tolerate wicked men, that you have tested those who claim to be apostles but are not, and have found them false. You have persevered and have endured hardships for my name, and have not grown weary. (vv. 2 & 3)

We can **summarise the praise under two headings**:

i. Determination in the face of hardship.

The Ephesian Christians were **hard workers** and the Lord commends them for this. The words used here are of backbreaking, sweat-inducing labour. Furthermore, they were not the types who, in a burst of enthusiasm put in a week's work then take a month's holiday. No, they were those who showed **perseverance and endurance**.

William Barclay comments that the Greek word **hupomene** is 'not the grim patience which resignedly accepts things, and which bows its head when troubles flow over it. Hupomone is the courageous gallantry which accepts suffering and hardship and loss and turns them in to grace and glory'.

And the **context** in which they exercised this endurance was one of **fierce persecution**. The church had been **born in suffering** – remember the riot at Ephesus instigated by the silversmith's trade union which led to Paul's departure from the city. And the church **grew up** in the same hostile climate – both from Imperial Rome during the terrible persecution by the Emperor Domitian and locally from civil and religious authorities, Jews and Gentiles.

In spite of all this, these Christians **kept going and kept working**. How we **need such people in our churches today** and how thankful we should be for those who have worked hard in the gospel to maintain the light on the lampstand. Far too many Christians are content to sit at ease in Zion and sing their favourite hymn:

'Jesus, I am resting, resting, resting..'

And how easily we **become discouraged when things get difficult**: despite the relative ease we face in the West when compared with the sufferings of many fellow-Christians throughout the world. That was **not the case with the Christians in Ephesus** and the **risen Lord commends them**, and **all those like them**, who **keep on going in the face of hardship**.

But that is **not all they were commended for** – determination in the face of hardship. . They were **also praised** by the Lord Jesus Christ for their

ii. Discrimination in the face of heresy
It is interesting and surely significant to recall Paul's final and moving appeal to the elders of the church at Ephesus. In it, he warns them of **dangers to come:**

Keep watch over yourselves and all the flock of which the Holy Spirit has made you overseers. Be shepherds of the church of God, which he bought with his own blood. I know that after I leave, savage wolves will come in among you and will not spare the flock. Even from your own number men will arise and distort the truth in order to draw away disciples after them. So be on your guard! Remember that for three years I never stopped warning each of you night and day with tears. (Acts 20:28–31)

His warnings were surely based on those of **Jesus himself** in the Sermon on the Mount when he told his disciples to watch out for *'wolves in sheep's clothing'* – false prophets (Matt. 7:15). It appears that leaders and church at Ephesus had **taken these warnings to heart**. *'Wolves'* had indeed come in among the scattered flocks of the Mediterranean world. Their false teaching ranged across the spectrum from **legalism** from Judaizers who sought to enforce the law of Moses on Gentile converts – to **license** from others from a Hellenistic background who sought to turn Christian liberty into an excuse for sexual indulgence and other excesses.

They are **described variously in these letters** to the seven churches as the Nicolaitans (later in verse 4, and in 2:15, in the letter to Pergamum), those who held to the 'teaching of Balaam' (2:14 – Pergamum;) and those who followed 'Jezebel' (2:20 – Thyatira). The exact details of each group, and whether in fact they are the same group, is uncertain.

What **is important** is that the Christians at Ephesus were not taken in by these people: they 'tested those who claim to be apostles but are not and have found them to be false' (v. 2). The **words of John himself** in his first Epistle had been applied in the local congregation:

> Dear friends, do not believe every spirit, but test the spirits to see whether they are from God, because many false prophets have gone out into the world. (1 John 4:1)

Now, I sense a **generational shift** in this area. I believe that people today are **less doctrinally aware** than they once were. Indeed, I suspect that you could preach heresy in many churches and not many people would know the difference.

I do not think this is just nostalgia on my part or purely anecdotal evidence. I have observed it in the doctrinal statements of missionary candidates and in my own preaching. Very rarely does anyone tackle me at the door over something I said. No doubt today will be an exception!

Perhaps much of this is the **spirit of the age in which we live** and a **reaction against a dead doctrinalism** which some of us also grew up with. But that is no excuse for no doctrine at all, and is it not significant that the church at Ephesus is **praised by the risen Lord for its 'intolerance'** of wicked men? This is no academic matter for the **life and future of the church of Jesus Christ is at stake here**. A man whose wife is being seduced by a plausible philanderer does not stand around in polite conversation with him. Such is the Lord's jealousy for his bride and his commendation of those who protect her integrity and purity.

So there is commendation for these Christians in Ephesus. **But then, abruptly and without warning, comes**

2.   CRITICISM (verse 4)
On the surface, it **seems such a small thing** when **weighed against all that was good** in the church at Ephesus. The praise lavished on Ephesus is more than any other church. If you were giving marks out of ten then I suppose you might have awarded them eight or nine!

But that is to look at things from a human perspective. The **Lord's diagnosis is that this one failing outweighs all the rest and is of acute seriousness.** Why? Because **this one thing will kill the church unless it is rectified**.

What is this terrible thing, this malaise within the ranks of the hard-working, preserving, orthodox church at Ephesus ?

Yet I hold this against you: You have forsaken your first love. (verse 4)

Commentators are uncertain as to whether this refers to their love for the Lord, their love for each other or their love for all people. In one sense, it is all of them but it **begins with a lack of love for the Lord**, which is the mainspring of all spiritual life. Once that goes, then **all other loves begin to suffer** and to wither and die.

Outwardly, all seemed well. If we had visited the church at Ephesus, we would have been highly impressed – lots of activity, sound Bible teaching, just the sort of church we would have gladly joined, a **model church** to all appearances – **save one**. The **Lord** with his piercing eyes **sees behind the facade** into the heart of the church and its members, and he removes the veil and **reveals that they have lost their first love**.

That love had been the **characteristic of the church at Ephesus** since its inception. The **letter to the Ephesians** is a letter of love, for the word is mentioned twenty three times in six chapters. John, their pastor, was above all else known as the **Apostle of love. His first Epistle** is full of the message of love, and he uses the word forty times in his three short Epistles.

But when John receives this message, **the church is forty years old**, middle-aged, and with many second-generation Christians. **Life may begin at forty but love may die at forty.**

So, **what remains when love dies in a church? Activity and orthodoxy**. And these things are usually the **characteristic of post first-generation churches and Christians**. It is interesting that **John the Apostle was known for two things** : for his love for the Lord and his fellow-Christians, and his hatred of false teaching and abhorrence of false teachers.

Two famous stories from church history about him illustrate this. It is said that when he was an old man, he was carried into church and all he repeated again and again was, *'Little children, love one another'*.

But there is also a story of John fleeing from a bathhouse on learning that Cerinthus, a well-known heretic, was also present in the establishment!

Somehow, he **kept the two things in balance – as does the Lord** when, after his criticism of the Ephesians in verse 4, he praises them for their hatred of heresy in verse 6. It should **not be either/ or but both/ and.** Unfortunately, fathers in the faith may be able to keep that balance, but **their children tend to lose the love and keep the hatred.**

Leon Morris comments on the Ephesians:

> They had yielded to the temptation, ever present in Christians, to put all their emphasis on sound teaching. In the process, they lost love, without which all else is nothing.

It **may be enough** for most people that a church is orthodox and hard-working, but it is **never enough** for the Lord for it communicates the wrong message to the world in which the church, any church is placed, and dishonours the one whose name we bear.

It is **so serious that the Lord would sooner close the church than to allow it to remain.** It is surely significant that it is only the first and last churches – Ephesus and Laodicea – which are threatened with closure by the risen Lord. In both cases, it is the loss of a burning love and zealous passion for the Lord which is the reason.

Now, if this is of s**uch vital importance to the Lord** it should also be of **vital importance to us.** Yet so often we are **more concerned about doctrinal orthodoxy and regular attendance at church and involvement in activities than our love for the Lord** – and so for each other. It is perhaps inevitable that **this love is the first thing to be lost and the hardest thing to maintain.** Like a marriage which has lost the fire of love between the partners, we still go through the motions and maintain a facade. That was the **state of the church in Ephesus.**

But only on one side. The **Lord's love for his people and for us is the same as ever** – and that is why he challenges us about this matter of vital importance – 'Do you truly love me?' It is **the most important question of all**, one which we should reflect on and seek to answer honestly before the Lord.

But the Lord is just like a doctor who offers an accurate diagnosis. Like a good doctor, the Great Physician **also offers a remedy,** for after criticism we then have:

3. CORRECTION (verse 5a)
The **remedy is in three parts:**
i. Remember:
He urges them to **think back to what they were,** to **look up and see how far they have fallen:**

> Remember the height from which you have fallen!

Many years ago, I remember **an occasion on holiday as a small child**. We were on the beach and had bought an inflatable lilo. I lay on it in the sea and looked up at the sky. Eventually, I dozed off, only to be wakened by distant cries. I sat up and saw to my horror that I had drifted far away from the shore. Quickly I paddled back to land. Good job the voice of my anxious parents had summoned me out of my reverie.

Few of us are **swept away from the moorings of faith by a tidal wave**. For most of us it is **a gradual drift**, imperceptible, bit by bit. How frightening it can be, therefore, when we are awakened by the Holy Spirit and **realise with horror how far we have drifted from our first love for the Lord**:

'If you had ever told me I would be like that when I first became a Christian, I would never have believed it.'

Yet that awakening and remembering are **essential steps on the road to recovery**. Think of **the Prodigal in the far country**. He started out with such high hopes and ended up in a pigsty eating swill. Yet it was there that he remembered:

'When he came to his senses, he said, 'How many of my father's hired men have food to spare, and here I am starving to death!' (Luke 15:17)

Maybe the Lord has **reminded us today of what we once were and how far we have fallen**. It may not be apparent to anyone else, for we are still active Christians and ardent defenders of the faith.

But like William Cowper we ask ourselves the question:

Where is the blessedness I knew,
When first I saw the Lord?
Where is the soul-refreshing view
Of Jesus and His Word?

Such remembering should be **a continuous exercise**, an **ongoing review**, for the tense of the verb is continuous – 'Keep on remembering!'

Then there is a **second step which follows from this**:

ii. Repent.

The verb here describes a **sharp and decisive act**. It means to agree with God's diagnosis of your condition, to admit your fault without qualification. The **words of repentance are always the same** – be they David in the Old Testament or the Prodigal in the New – **'I have sinned against the Lord.'**

Repentance is a change of mind, a turning towards God. It is not just saying the words but **putting them into action.** The Prodigal said, 'I will arise and go to my Father..' and so he **'arose and went'**

Maybe this is a **decisive day for you** – when you **repent.**

And there is a **third thing which follows**

Remember the height from which you have fallen! Repent and **do the things you did at first....***(verse 5)*

iii. Repeat

What were the things you did at first, when you first repented and responded to God's wonderful love in the Lord Jesus Christ:

> · you loved to spend time with him
> · you loved to read his Word and listen to his voice
> · you loved to be with God's people
> · you loved to serve the Lord

These things are the fruits of repentance. But the **key word is** *'loved'.* All these things you **did out of love not duty.** Like a marriage where the fervour has gone, the facade is maintained only by an image in which things are done out of duty alone. What we **need above all else is a fresh love for the Lord Jesus Christ.**

Maybe we **think that is an impossibility** – and it is humanly speaking. But the one who placed his love first in our hearts through the Holy Spirit (Rom. 5:5) can also **renew it when we turn to him.**

When we set off down the road of repentance, back to the Father and home, we find that **our poor and fickle love is met by his great and unchanging love.** He is already looking out for us and he runs to meet us. He **greets us with joy and forgiveness and restoration.**

The son said to him, 'Father, I have sinned against heaven and against you. I am no longer worthy to be called your son.'

'**But the father** said to his servants, 'Quick! Bring the best robe and put it on him. Put a ring on his finger and sandals on his feet. Bring the fattened calf and kill it. Let's have a feast and celebrate. For this son of mine was dead and is alive again; he was lost and is found.' So they began to celebrate. (Luke 15:21–24)

That is **what God offers to us – now and eternally.** The letter to Ephesus contains a **great promise of eternal fellowship with God:**

To him who overcomes, I will give the right to eat from the tree of life, which is in the paradise of God. (verse 7)

Adam, in the first Paradise before the Fall was **forbidden to eat of the tree of life**. But the **Christian is promised that privilege**. The word used for 'tree' here is an unusual one, used in the New Testament to describe the cross of Jesus, by which he became a curse so that we might enjoy the blessing of eternal fellowship with God – not the wages of sin but the gift of God which is eternal life through Jesus Christ our Lord. This is **promised to those who overcome through Christ who has overcome**.

But with the promise is **a warning** and a choice with no middle road – **only a stark alternative.** *Remember the height from which you have fallen! Repent and do the things you did at first.* **If you do not repent, I will come to you and remove your lampstand from its place.** *(verse 5)*

The **warning is imminent** – literally, 'I am coming'. Sadly, the lampstand was removed from Ephesus. Church and city are buried, literally, in the sands of time. Barclay comments:

Its crowded harbour is now a marsh, six miles from the sea, and its thronging streets are now a waste and desolation.'

And, we might add, its **songs of praise are silent**, its **light of witness has long gone out**.

We **cannot presume on God's blessings on our churches**. Many buildings are now derelict or taken over by commercialism and even other religions. The **only way to ensure a bright and constant witness in every generation is to stay in love with the Lord, and to heed his warnings**:

Yet I hold this against you: You have **forsaken your first love.**
He who has an ear, let him hear what the Spirit says.